# Make the Right Move
## Buying and Selling Your Home Successfully

# Make the Right Move
## Buying and Selling Your Home Successfully

# Nicki Household

### Foreword by Emma Basden and Jason Maloney

**Nicki Household** is a freelance writer and specialist in consumer affairs. She writes about lifestyle, property and financial issues for a wide range of national magazines and has written publications to accompany several BBC television series, including *All the Right Moves*. In two decades of journalism she has been a regular contributor to *Radio Times, The Times* and *Sunday Times, Woman's Weekly,* the *Daily Mail* and the *Times Educational Supplement.* Her knowledge of the property market goes far beyond the theoretical as she has bought, done up and sold eight London houses.

**Emma Basden** is an estate agent with over ten years' experience. She began her career in the prestigious Park Lane offices of Foxtons and quickly moved on to manage a lettings department in Notting Hill Gate. After a further three years as manager of Winkworth Agency in Islington, Emma ventured out on her own to start the successful MySpace Agency in Islington.

**Jason Maloney** has had a varied and colourful career that includes promoting bands and working in advertising. For the past ten years, however, he has worked solely in the building trade and now operates a successful family-run construction business.

This book is published to accompany the BBC series *Safe as Houses*, which was first broadcast on BBC2 in 2004.
Series Producer: Pete Lawrence
Executive producer: Mark Hill

Published by BBC Books, BBC Worldwide Ltd
Woodlands
80 Wood Lane
London W12 0TT

First published 2004
Copyright © BBC Worldwide 2004
Foreword copyright © Emma Basden and Jason Maloney 2004
The moral right of the authors has been asserted

ISBN: 0 563 48773 9

Commissioning Editor: Rachel Copus
Project Editor: Warren Albers
Copy Editor: Christine King
Art Director: Sarah Ponder
Design: Grade Design Consultants
Picture Researcher: Victoria Hall
Production Controller: Arlene Alexander

Set in Helvetica Neue and OCRB
Printed and bound in France by Imprimerie Pollina, s.a - n° L91878.

BBC Worldwide would like to thank the following for providing photographs and permission to reproduce copyright material. While every effort has been made to trace and acknowledge all copyright holders, we would like to apologize should there have been any errors or omissions.
Alamy 22, 92,150; BBC Worldwide/Andy Woods 125; Craig Easton 6; Foxtons 70; Getty Images 2, 10, 44, 112.

# Contents

A TASTEFULLY PRESENTED PERIOD
FAMILY HOUSE OFFERING FOUR LARGE
BEDROOMS IN A QUIET ROAD WITHIN
THE POPULAR BEDFORD PARK AREA

102 WOODSTOCK ROAD, CHISWICK W4

* Four Double Bedrooms
* Period Features
* Short Walk to High Road
* Oven
* Secluded

# Foreword

**Selling one house and buying another can be a daunting experience.** Once you've stepped onto the property ladder, you'll know that a wrong move can leave you feeling like an emotional wreck. Add to this the horror stories about house-buying from friends, neighbours and the media, and you might wonder whether it's a pursuit best avoided. But when everything goes smoothly (and, believe it or not, it *can* happen that way), moving house will give you a huge sense of achievement and open up a new world of possibilities.

The television series *Safe as Houses* gave us the chance to follow ten families through the highs and lows of house-buying as they tried to find that perfect property. As professionals involved in various aspects of the trade, we understand how the buying and selling of property *ought* to go. But the series reminded us just what an emotional rollercoaster it can be. We've been there for the thrill when everything fits into place and a family's life changes as they move into that dream home. We've also been a shoulder to cry on when problem after problem and crisis after crisis have made our participants wonder why they ever started the whole process in the first place.

The one thing we've taken away from all this is that it's vital to be able to plan ahead for the best (and the worst) that can happen to you. It will help to avoid some of the misery if you take time in advance to think through what you want and need, to know what your options are at every stage, and to understand what other people are talking about. You won't be able to prepare for everything, but if you know what to expect, you'll stay ahead of the game every step of the way.

This book to accompany the series is a real gem – a practical and simple guide leading you step-by-step through the whole process of buying and selling property. It may not be a shoulder to cry on when those inevitable problems do crop up, but it will be there to give you all the tools, facts and figures you need to sail through. Even when the going gets rough, the information in this book should help you deal confidently with each obstacle. It's the next best thing to a couple of professionals on hand to lend advice when you need it the most.

Emma Basden and Jason Maloney, September 2003

# Introduction

**Our homes are the most expensive things we ever buy – and the mortgages we saddle ourselves with to pay for them are the biggest financial burdens of our lives.** The aim of this book is to guide you through the minefield of buying and selling property and help you choose the right home for your lifestyle and the best mortgage for your financial situation. It also includes essential advice on repairs, renovation and home improvements, helping you to avoid costly mistakes and maximize your home's value.

As everyone who has done it knows, buying or selling a home is a roller-coaster ride. Finding a place you like and can afford is never easy and, even when you've finally tracked down the house or flat of your dreams, so many things can go pear-shaped. Someone outbids or 'gazumps' you, you can't sell your own property, your 'rock-solid' buyer backs out, or your dream home turns out to be riddled with damp, dry rot and woodworm. Anxious moments are part and parcel of every property transaction. But even though moving house can be stressful (second only to death and divorce, it's said), it is also exciting, rewarding and fun. More of us than ever – about two-thirds of the population – now own the homes we live in. We do so because property is a solid investment and we like the feeling of security. We also enjoy having the freedom to improve, extend, redecorate and make the place an expression of ourselves and our lifestyle.

Around 1.5 million homes are bought and sold in the UK each year and, whatever pundits say about bubbles bursting and markets bottoming out, property has remained a reliable investment for several decades. Even when there was a sharp drop in property values back in 1989/90, it was chiefly a disaster for home-owners who had recently taken out a very high mortgage and had to sell during the period when they were in negative equity (when their mortgage debt was greater than the value of the property). The real problem then was not the drop in house prices but the simultaneous rise in interest rates. People with big loans couldn't afford their hugely increased mortgage payments and so, in some cases, their homes were repossessed. But the vast majority of home-owners were unaffected and property prices soon started to rise again.

Since the average house price rose an astonishing 25 per cent in the financial year to April 2003, while the value of the average shares portfolio dropped 30 per cent, it's not surprising that so many people are now raising mortgages in order to buy to let, or investing in property to provide future pensions. But recent price rises have been exceptional – the average annual house-price rise between 1970 and 1995 was a more modest 4.7 per cent. No one can guarantee that house prices will continue to rise in the near future, but in the long term it does seem a good bet.

However, not everyone has gained from the situation. Even though mortgages are cheaper than they have been for decades, in some areas of the country, especially London and the South East, it has become virtually impossible for young people on average incomes to find a first home they can afford. According to the Council of Mortgage Lenders, first-time buyers now account for only a third of all mortgage lending, compared with around a half in 1988, and their average age (29 in 1974) has risen to 34.

The average first-time-buyer house price is now £98,000 in the UK as a whole (and £170,000 in Greater London), compared with £75,000 in 1996 (*source:* Halifax). As a result, many young Londoners who are at the stage when they should be able to buy a home of their own are still sharing a rented flat with friends or strangers, renting a room, or living at home with parents – and large student debts only add to the problem. Possible ways round this, such as buying with friends and housing association shared-ownership schemes, are outlined in Chapter 2.

When Home Information Packs (see page 86) become compulsory, probably in 2006, the buying and selling process will, everybody hopes, be speeded up. At the moment it is far too long and complicated (except in Scotland, which has its own system), because there are so many different stages after an offer has been accepted. You might think the whole process could be accomplished in just a few weeks, but it usually takes two to three months. Occasionally, if it's a cash purchase and both sides are in a real hurry, a sale can be completed in four weeks, but certain things seem to take for ever. Common causes of delay include 'chain' hold-ups (when your buyer or seller is having problems with their own buyer or seller), mortgage lenders dragging their feet and complications caused by surveys or local authority searches.

Then there are all the hardened professionals you have to deal with – estate agents, solicitors, surveyors, financial advisers and mortgage lenders – not to mention assorted vendors and purchasers (buyers and sellers, to you and me). And not all of these, alas, will be friendly and helpful. But this book will help you find your way confidently through the home-buying maze, so the whole process, from viewing to moving, can be as enjoyable and stress-free as possible.

# 1

# Before you start

**People move house for a wide variety of reasons. Families may need more space or a bigger garden.** Young people want to leave the parental home or move on from shared accommodation. Retired people may want to relocate to the country or be nearer their families. We also have to find new homes when we get married or start new jobs, and when we start (or stop) living with someone. But not all moves are prompted by major life events. Sometimes people just fancy an upgrade, a new lifestyle or a change of scene.

# Rent or buy?

**Whatever your reason for moving, often the first question that arises is: should you rent or should you buy?**

However desirable home-ownership may seem, it has a downside as well as an upside. A home, like a dog, is not just for Christmas, it's for life – or a large chunk of it. Once you own one, you will be solely responsible for its upkeep, inside and out. That means new roofs, new boilers, new kitchens and bathrooms, new floors, redecoration, updates, replacements, repairs, maintenance and insurance. Unlike a tenant, you can never be sure quite how much owning a home will cost you because no one can foresee a structural calamity like subsidence – when the ground under your house gradually caves in and cracks appear in the walls (don't worry, it's quite rare) – or a sudden sharp rise in mortgage interest rates.

Buying is not right for everyone, but it's an excellent idea for people who:
- have a regular income
- have saved enough to put down a sizeable deposit (100 per cent mortgages are available, but cost more)
- feel it's important to own the place they live in
- feel ready to take on the responsibilities of home-ownership – repairs, monthly mortgage payments and all
- are keen to put down roots in an area and live there for some time
- like the idea of investing in their own home and perhaps making money by improving it, selling it on or letting out rooms.

But buying a house or flat is an expensive business, so it would certainly make more sense to rent if you know you are going to have to up sticks within a year or so. Even if the value of your property goes up in that time, you won't make anything if you sell too soon, because your profit will be eaten up by moving expenses – the valuation, survey, stamp duty, legal costs, furniture removal, and any essential building work, carpets, curtains or appliances needed in your new home.

Renting a home involves fewer responsibilities and is, of course, the only option if you can't get a mortgage. But when you rent, the money you pay is contributing to someone else's investment, not your own. And if you're renting from a private landlord, you're very much at his/her mercy. Landlords don't always keep their properties in a good state of repair, and they can chuck you out when the lease ends or if they want to sell the place or live in it themselves. Structural alterations are out of the question and you can't even redecorate a room without the landlord's permission.

When you buy a home, on the other hand, your monthly payments (though mostly interest at first) gradually increase your equity in the property (the proportion of its value that you own outright). You can also do whatever you like to the interior layout and colour scheme, and you have security of tenure – no one can chuck you out of your home unless you fall so behind with your mortgage payments that the property is repossessed by a bank or building society.

Buying is also cheaper at the moment, because mortgage interest rates are so low. You do of course have to find that substantial initial deposit but, unless your mortgage is truly vast, your monthly mortgage payments will probably be lower than rent payments to a private landlord. A mortgage is also cheaper over the long term because inflation gradually reduces the real cost of your mortgage payments, so after five or ten years they take up a smaller share of your income. Rents, on the other hand, keep going up, so you never feel better off.

Renting from a social landlord such as a local authority or housing association is probably the cheapest and most protected way of putting a roof over your head, especially if you are likely to become unemployed – but you have be in real need to be considered. Once there, you will have good security of tenure but no financial investment – unless you later get an opportunity to purchase the property at a discount, as an existing council tenant (see Chapter 2).

## Summary

### Advantages of renting
- You have no responsibility for maintenance and repairs.
- A smaller deposit is required (usually one month's rent).
- You have no long-term financial commitment.
- You can move quickly.

### Disadvantages of renting
- You have no financial investment – the rent money is gone for good.
- You can be forced to move out when your lease ends or after a statutory period of notice.
- You can't make major improvements. Even if you obtain permission, any increase in the value of the property will benefit only the landlord.

## Advantages of buying

- Cheaper monthly outlay – but this may not always be the case. In the 1980s, when interest rates were high and there was no shortage of rented accommodation, it was cheaper to rent than buy.
- A long-term investment that will keep pace, at least, with inflation (the cost of living). The housing boom of recent years has made it seem as if property is a sure-fire investment, but there's no guarantee that this situation will continue. Don't forget that everyone else's property has gone up too, so unless you plan to downsize or go to a much cheaper area next time you move, your profits will have to be ploughed into your next home.
- Useful equity. As the value of your home increases over the years, the money you have locked up in it – your equity – can be used in a number of ways. Banks may be willing to lend money against it, for example to help you start a business, or funds could be released to provide an additional pension. However, equity-release pension schemes should be chosen with considerable caution, and only after independent financial advice, as they are weighted heavily in favour of the companies that offer them.
- More choice of property styles: old or new, a house or a flat, top floor or basement, detached, terraced or semi-detached, and with or without a garden. You might want a run-down place that's ideal for creative conversion, or one that's ready to move straight into. Your only restriction is price.
- Security of tenure – no one can get you out.
- More choice of location. When renting, you tend to have to settle for what's available. As a buyer, you are free to pinpoint the areas you like and can afford, and only consider properties in those areas.
- Freedom to do what you like to your home. When you own your home, you can do what you like to it, subject to planning permission, building regulations and (for historic buildings only) listed building consent. You can knock down walls, move bathrooms and kitchens, choose outlandish colour schemes or turn the place into a shrine to Elvis. Subject to planning permission, you can extend down into the cellar, up into the loft, over the garage or out into the garden. You can also paint the exterior any colour you like (unless it's a conservation area), though you may make some enemies!

## Disadvantages of buying

- The buying process is expensive, although less so if you can find a home for £60,000 or less and avoid stamp duty.
- If mortgage rates rise, so will your monthly payments.
- You can't move house quickly.
- You are responsible for the maintenance of your property.

# Property prices

**Since October 1997, house prices have increased by a national average of 64.4 per cent.** But this varies wildly from region to region, with a rise of just 12.5 per cent in Scotland, 54.7 per cent in the East Midlands and a staggering 90.8 per cent in Greater London, where the average house price is now £195,391 (*source:* Halifax). The South West and East Anglia have also seen rises of over 80 per cent. The overall average buying price of a UK property is now around £110,000.

Like most other prices, property prices are influenced by supply and demand. The greater the demand, the higher the price. There is still a housing shortage in areas like London, the South East and East Anglia, whereas in some areas in the North – especially those that have suffered industrial decline – there is a surplus.

The prices within any given area are determined by:

- location
- size of the property and size of the garden
- architectural style and type of property
- structural condition
- standard of decor and how well a property is presented
- length of lease (if not freehold).

Planning developments can also have a huge effect. New roads, railway lines and motorways (not to mention airports) bring prices down if they are too close, but can raise values if they bring transport benefits without raising noise levels or being an eyesore. A bypass that takes traffic away from a town will boost local values – except for properties that now have a nice view of the bypass. Values are also affected by building developments, especially when they spoil views or change the character of an area. No wonder the NIMBY (Not In My Back Yard) attitude prevails!

Legislation and economic policy can also affect property values. Prices go up if buying becomes easier – for example when 'right to buy' legislation and alterations to leasehold laws enabled tenants to buy the freeholds of their homes, or when mortgage interest rates are low. But they go down if buying becomes harder, as when mortgage interest rates go up. In other words, when people are confident about buying, prices go up, but when they're nervous, prices stand still or go down. There are also seasonal fluctuations. Most people buy in the spring, early summer or autumn, so you're more likely to find a bargain during the winter or the school summer holidays.

# The property professionals

**Before you launch yourself into the property market, it's worth knowing what all the different people who make their living from property actually do.**

### Estate agents

Estate agents value properties, advertise them, draw them to the attention of suitable buyers and negotiate sales. Some also arrange mortgages and insurance, and offer complete relocation packages. Their commission, paid by the seller, is normally between 1 and 3 per cent of the selling price.

### Solicitors (or licensed conveyancers)

Solicitors manage the legal side of buying and selling property – the conveyancing.

### Chartered surveyors

Chartered surveyors undertake valuations, home-buyers' reports and structural surveys. They also oversee building projects.

### Architects

Architects design and draw up detailed plans for new buildings, and for alterations and extensions to existing ones.

### Banks and building societies

These finance your property purchase (or self-build project) with a mortgage loan. How much you can borrow and at what interest rate depends on your income, your deposit, your credit-worthiness and the value of the property.

### Independent mortgage brokers

These tell you about the different kinds of mortgage available and offer advice on which is the best one for you. Banks and building societies are not independent mortgage brokers as they recommend only their own products.

### Property developers

Property developers buy property, then do it up to sell or rent out.

### House builders

House builders put up new houses and developments to sell.

# A bird's-eye view of costs

Moving house costs an alarming amount because you have to pay substantial sums not only to many of the above-named professionals, but also to the government (stamp duty), local authorities (searches), removal men and so on – in general, the higher the value of the property, the steeper the costs.

## Buying costs

What follows is a breakdown of the various types of cost you may be faced with when buying a property. Not all the costs apply to every purchase – there's more detail about all these charges, and when they apply, in later chapters.

### Your deposit

This is ideally 10 per cent of the purchase price if you want to take advantage of the best mortgage interest rates. Some lenders let you borrow 100 per cent of the property's value, but this will probably mean paying a higher interest rate and a mortgage indemnity premium to protect the lender.

### Mortgage costs

Some lenders get away with charging much more than others, but you may be asked to pay:

- an arrangement fee of between £100 and £350
- an application fee of £100 to £300 (this is often refunded on completion of the mortgage)
- a mortgage indemnity premium. This protects the lender if you are borrowing a high percentage of the value of the property, and is 4, 6 or 8 per cent of the amount borrowed above 75 per cent of the purchase price. You can add it to the loan, but you will then pay interest on it for the life of the mortgage.

### Solicitor's fees

Solicitors usually charge a flat fee for doing all the legal work involved in your purchase and keeping you advised throughout the transaction. Fees start at around £350 plus VAT.

## Disbursements

These include land registry fees, local searches and other fees and searches: usually £400 to £500.

## Stamp duty

This is a tax you pay the government for the privilege of buying a home. It is payable on all property costing more than £60,000 and goes up in steps:

- up to £60,000: nil
- £60,001–£250,000: 1 per cent
- £250,001–£500,000: 3 per cent
- £500,000+: 4 per cent

Ten years ago, relatively few first-time buyers fell into the stamp duty bracket, as it was only in London that the average first-time buyer had to pay more than £60,000 for a home. Now, due to price rises, first-time buyers in six UK regions are paying stamp duty that amounts to between 2.8 per cent and 5 per cent of their annual earnings. Since the government is now receiving nearly four times as much in stamp duty (some £2.5 billion) than in 1996/7, it is a classic stealth tax. Price rises have also drawn a great many far-from-wealthy home-owners into the inheritance-tax bracket.

## Survey cost

This varies from about £250 for a valuation report to around £400 for a home-buyer's survey and upwards of £500 for a full structural survey. Some mortgage lenders refund the cost of a valuation.

## Removal costs

These depend on how much is being moved. A removal firm will base their quote on how long they think it will take to complete the loading and unloading. If you ask them to do the packing, it will cost more. Costs vary from around £300 for moving the contents of a small flat a short distance, to several thousand for moving the contents of a large house a long way. You'll save a lot if you hire a van and do it yourself, but it may not be worth it if it means carrying large, heavy items up or down several flights of stairs.

## Storage

You will only have to pay for this if you have to move out of your old home before you move into your new one. It can be included in the removal quote, or, if the company doesn't provide this service, space in a storage facility costs upwards of £120 a month.

### Moving-in costs

These depend on what needs doing to make your new home functional – plumbing-in, connection and disconnection of gas and electrical appliances, essential repairs, change of address cards, and mail forwarding.

### Essential purchases

These include carpets, curtains, furniture, appliances and so on.

## Selling costs

The cost of selling your home will depend on whether you use an estate agent, and how much you spend on getting the property ready to sell. See Chapter 8 for tips on how to add inexpensive buyer-appeal to your home.

### Getting your home ready to sell

This costs mainly time and energy, but you may have to buy some paint, a large plant pot or two and some cheerful rugs and throws.

### Estate agent's fees

These are the biggest cost of selling a home. Most estate agents charge a fixed percentage of the selling price. If you drive a hard bargain, some will agree to 1 per cent as long as they are sole agents. Multiple-agency costs vary from 2 per cent to 3 per cent of the sale price. Selling at auction costs about 2.5 per cent of the sale price. There may be other charges, especially if the house is not sold.

### Advertising costs

These will apply if you sell privately – classified ads, a double-sided 'For Sale' sign (around £50), property website fees. Some sites are free, so you could get away with selling your home for nothing.

### Solicitor's fees

These are slightly less for a sale than for a purchase and start at around £250, depending on the value of the property. There are virtually no disbursements involved in a property sale.

## Work out the cost

Even if you pare these costs down to a minimum, moving isn't cheap. It really makes sense to know in advance exactly how much your move is going to cost, so once you've got all your quotes and estimates add them up to make a total. Hopefully it won't make you decide to stay put!

**Buying costs**

Deposit: _____

Mortgage fees: _____

Legal/conveyancing fees: _____

Removal costs: _____

Moving-in costs: _____

**Total (buying):** _____

**Selling costs**

Estate agent: _____

Legal fees: _____

Improvements to property: _____

**Total (selling):** _____

*Total (buying and selling):* _____

The following three tables, taken from the 2002 Woolwich Cost of Moving Survey, will give you a fair idea of the costs of buying, selling or upgrading your home.

| Buying costs (£s) in England and Wales (2002) | | | | | |
|---|---|---|---|---|---|
| House price | Solicitor | Land registry | Searches | Stamp duty | Total |
| 25,000 | 434 | 40 | 144 | 0 | **618** |
| 50,000 | 409 | 60 | 144 | 0 | **613** |
| 60,000 | 417 | 60 | 144 | 0 | **621** |
| 80,000 | 436 | 100 | 144 | 800 | **1,480** |
| 100,000 | 463 | 100 | 144 | 1,000 | **1,707** |
| 150,000 | 523 | 200 | 144 | 1,500 | **2,367** |
| 200,000 | 571 | 200 | 144 | 2,000 | **2,915** |
| 300,000 | 699 | 300 | 144 | 9,000 | **10,143** |
| 500,000 | 899 | 300 | 144 | 15,000 | **16,343** |
| 750,000 | 1,225 | 500 | 144 | 30,000 | **31,869** |
| 1,000,000 | 1,627 | 500 | 144 | 40,000 | **42,271** |

| Selling costs (£s) in England and Wales (2002) | | | |
| --- | --- | --- | --- |
| House price | Solicitor | Estate agent | Total |
| 25,000 | 381 | 728 | **1,109** |
| 50,000 | 396 | 936 | **1,332** |
| 60,000 | 399 | 1,020 | **1,419** |
| 80,000 | 422 | 1,253 | **1,675** |
| 100,000 | 446 | 1,490 | **1,936** |
| 150,000 | 502 | 2,129 | **2,631** |
| 200,000 | 551 | 2,851 | **3,402** |
| 300,000 | 658 | 4,132 | **4,790** |
| 500,000 | 867 | 6,697 | **7,564** |
| 750,000 | 1,157 | 9,843 | **11,000** |
| 1,000,000 | 1,547 | 13,080 | **14,627** |

| Cost (£s) of upgrading home in England and Wales | | | |
| --- | --- | --- | --- |
| These total costs include solicitor, estate agent, land registry, searches and stamp duty. | | | |
| Price of existing home | Price of new home | Cost 2001 | Cost 2002 |
| 60,000 | 100,000 | 3,195 | 3,126 |
| 80,000 | 150,000 | 4,167 | 4,042 |
| 100,000 | 150,000 | 4,499 | 4,303 |
| 100,000 | 200,000 | 5,080 | 4,851 |
| 200,000 | 300,000 | 14,009 | 13,545 |
| 300,000 | 500,000 | 21,921 | 39,433 |

# 2

# What to buy and where

**We all probably have an idea of the kind of place we'd buy if we won the lottery but, in the real world, you have to reconcile what you need and want with what you can afford.** This means establishing your priorities and deciding what compromises you are, or are not, prepared to make.

Decisions have to made about:

- general location – country, town, village or suburbs
- precise location – specific areas, specific roads or developments
- type of property – house or flat
- style of property – detached, terraced, ground floor, penthouse
- space – number of bedrooms, size of living area, separate workspace
- outdoor space – garden, patio, balcony, roof terrace
- essential local amenities – park, shops, schools, transport, gym
- your journey(s) to work – how easy, how long
- nearness to family and friends
- soundness of investment – likelihood of value going up.

The trick (as with so many things) is to have your priorities firmly in place, but not to be too rigid about them. Properties may come up that are not at all what you thought you wanted, but that would actually suit you to a T.

# Location

**Nothing, as estate agents love to tell us, influences prices and values as much as location.** In short, it doesn't matter how beautifully done up a house or flat is if it's on a noisy, polluted road, backing on to the town dump. Even if you like a particular property so much that you decide you don't mind these blights, a lot of other buyers will mind them, so the place will be difficult to sell. Generally speaking, a smaller, less well-done-up property in a charming, blight-free area would be a much better buy.

Before starting to house-hunt, it's important to familiarize yourself with the area. This can be difficult if you are relocating to another part of the country, but it really is essential to spend time in the town or area you're going to live in, and get a feel for it. Look in estate agents' windows to get an idea of local prices, pay visits to the districts, streets or villages that seem possible. This is doubly important if you're moving to a new environment and a new lifestyle, as sometimes the reality doesn't match the dream.

## The rural idyll

Town-dwellers often long for a new life in the country. You may picture a charming little house or cottage, surrounded by woods and fields – chickens, pets, a vegetable garden and only the sounds of nature to interrupt your peace. It's a lovely idea but one that needs very careful consideration if you have no experience of country life.

The countryside isn't all birdsong and trotting ponies. Rural landscapes can seem very bleak and lonely on a rainy day, especially if you're used to the hum and activity of living in town. Many is the townie who has come scurrying back to the big smoke after only a few months of rural bliss because they can't stand the isolation and lack of amenities.

Town and country people are not the same. To live happily in the country, it helps to have some rural interests and be fairly self-sufficient. One woman who moved back to London after little more than a year in Norfolk admits she kept making unnecessary trips to the supermarket, just to be surrounded by people. Villages can be friendly places, but it sometimes takes years for an outsider to be accepted as part of the community – despite how it seems in *The Archers*! So if you're not 100 per cent sure that rural life is for you, start by letting your property in town and renting one in the country. If you're a first-time buyer, think about renting before you buy. That way, you won't have burnt your bridges if you decide to move back to town. Remember that prices are higher and rise faster in cities. If you sell your town property and then want to move back, you may no longer be able to afford the kind of home you had before. Of course, reversing the decision to live in the country isn't so easy if it would mean changing children's schools again or finding a new job but, if you've hung on to your town property, at least you won't be seriously out of pocket.

If your heart is firmly set on country life, try to do your viewing in winter, so you get a more realistic picture. Do bear in mind that:

- big gardens are hard work and outbuildings require maintenance
- silence, pure air and sweet smells can't be taken for granted. Find out what neighbouring land is used for
- if you don't have mains sewerage, there'll be a cesspit that needs emptying every year. If there's no mains water, your water supply will need to be analysed
- there may be public footpaths that go right past your property
- a house with beautiful views may get buffeted by howling winds in rough weather
- if there's any risk of flooding from a river or estuary, choose a property on high ground. Elevated but sheltered is best.

But the country is your place if you are looking for an old building such as a barn, a school or church to convert. And, of course, it's where most people look for a second home or 'country cottage'. Different criteria obviously apply if a property is used only as a weekend retreat. Isolation and lack of amenities become a positive advantage, though it still makes sense to choose somewhere that won't get flooded in spring or cut off by snow in winter.

## RURAL IDYLL – CASE STUDY

**West Londoners Clare and Jim D always intended to move to the country when their children grew up and left home. Having both been raised in rural communities, they felt they wanted that way of life for their retirement. But when the moment came it was a much harder decision than they thought. After 20 years in the same house, much of their social life revolved around local friends. Clare was a leading light in the amateur dramatic society, and they were used to having good shops, restaurants and theatres on their doorstep.**

But the lure of country life was strong so they went ahead and put their Chiswick house on the market. Soon there was a serious offer on the table and that was when they began to wonder if they were burning their bridges. Suppose life in a little West Country village didn't live up to their expectations – would they be able to afford to move back to London? Clare and Jim wisely decided to put their Chiswick house with a letting agent and find somewhere to rent in Dorset. Then, if they changed their minds, they would be able to move back to town without losing too much money.

Rural life did, in fact, agree with them and two years later they sold the London house and bought a cottage in Dorset. But it worked out even better than they hoped, because London prices had increased so much in the meantime that they were able to buy a small investment flat in Chiswick as well.

## Living in a town or city

In terms of lifestyle, there is a big difference between inner cities and suburbs – almost as big as between town and country. Suburbs are quieter, cleaner, calmer (and much more boring, some would say!). Families like them because they offer more garden and living space, amenities are good and there's often a strong sense of community which makes it easy for both children and parents to make local friends. At the same time, there's not the nosiness of an isolated country village (though some people love this).

Inner cities, on the other hand, are noisy, buzzy, exciting, multicultural. Some inner-city locales offer bright lights and sophistication, others are still poor and run-down, most are somewhere between the two or on their way up. Inner-city life is great if you're hip and trendy, and if you look in the right places you'll be able to buy something cheap(ish) and hopefully watch it go up in value.

Wherever you live in a town, you will probably be reasonably near public transport, shops, schools and health care. There's also a wider choice of homes than in rural areas. In a big town you'll find studio flats, converted flats, purpose-built flats, two-up-one-down terraced cottages, Edwardian and Victorian semi-detached houses, and all sorts of new housing developments from warehouse conversions to modern apartment blocks and new family houses.

## Find the next up-and-coming area

A great many districts that used to be considered 'shabby' are now sprouting conservatories and loft conversions because there's a serious shortage of middle-range housing in Britain. Of course, it takes several years for the character of a neighbourhood to change completely, but it's the first people to move in who make the most money. The only disadvantage is that you have to wait a while for good shops and restaurants – and other 'improvers' – to appear.

The best bargains are to be found in areas that are about to be discovered. These often lie right next door to areas that are already up-and-coming but, to qualify, they must be attractive in their own right and have real 'potential' – quiet streets with appealing house styles and with no obvious drawbacks like run-down estates or grim-looking factories.

What matters most, though, is that you choose an area you like and where you will enjoy living. The only reason for buying a home in a place you don't like is if you are acquiring the property purely to do it up and sell it. In that case, your only criteria will be the value and buyer-appeal of the property after you've improved it. If you're buying to let, your criteria will be different again. In this case, you want a property that's easily maintained and eminently lettable – for example, a modern flat in a convenient location (see Chapter 7 for more information about buying to let).

# Types of property

**Your future home could be old and full of character or brand new and waiting for you to stamp it with your own distinctive style.** Before you begin your property search, it's worth taking a bit of time to consider not only your personal taste, but also your practical needs.

## Very old houses

Houses that are more than, say, 150 years old are much sought after, especially if they have a romantic inglenook fireplace and exposed beams. They are also charming and fun to live in. Georgian houses (built 1714–1830), with their neo-classical simplicity, are particularly elegant. But unless you are into doing up wrecks (see below and Chapter 7), it's best to choose one that has already been well modernized – replumbed, rewired, rethatched, timber-treated, damp-proofed and with a good bathroom and kitchen. Even the best old houses develop problems, but if an old property has been neglected for a long time it can cost a fortune to put it right.

## Listed buildings

There are some 370,000 listed buildings in England, 46,000 in Scotland. 26,000 in Wales and 8,500 in Northern Ireland. Buildings are listed when they are of special architectural or historic interest. All buildings built before 1700 are listed, as are most built between 1700 and 1840 and a few from later periods. Buildings given a Grade 1 or Grade 2* listing by English Heritage are really very special and you can't change anything, inside or out, without permission. English Heritage grants are sometimes available for urgent repairs. The vast majority of listed buildings are Grade 2 (without a star), which means they are 'of special interest, warranting every effort to preserve them'.

If you are lucky enough to buy a Grade 2 listed house or cottage, there will be limitations on what you can and can't do to it. For example, if you need to replace the windows you must use traditional wooden window frames, not some other material. Some very old buildings need to be painted with limewash and distemper because modern plastic paints stop the bricks 'breathing'. If your mortgage lender insists on a chemical damp-course, you will have to make sure this is allowed.

Any interior or exterior repairs and alterations that might change the character of the building need listed building consent from the local council. In practice, a conservation officer can often tell you in advance whether your proposals are likely to be accepted. Carrying out unauthorized work on a listed building is a criminal offence, and you can be made to put everything back the way it was.

The Society for the Protection of Ancient Buildings publishes a quarterly list (available to members) of listed buildings in need of repair that are for sale.

## Victorian/Edwardian houses

The Victorians built roughly a third of all existing British houses so, if a Victorian house is what you want, it shouldn't be too hard to find. Victorian properties vary in size from tiny cottages to substantial family homes. Victorian town houses tend to be tall and thin as, at the time they were built, it was the servants and not the owners who had to keep running up and down stairs.

What people love about Victorian, and also Edwardian, houses is the generous way they were built – their high ceilings, period features and the opportunities they offer for stylish modernization. Even two-up-two-downs were finished with an attention to detail that would be unimaginable these days. Unfortunately, many were the subject of horrendous 'improvements' in the 1950s and 1960s – fireplaces ripped out, panelled doors replaced with flush ones, window styles changed and so on.

These features can be put back, at a price, but it would be far better to find a property that still has as many as possible of its original fireplaces, doors, windows, banisters, ceiling cornices and mouldings, dados and picture rails. Look out for houses that still have their generous hallways and well-proportioned rooms.

## 1930s estates

The 1930s are a neglected period of housing that is quietly staging a comeback. Thirties houses used to be seen as having neither the charm of older houses nor the convenience of new ones, but their advantages have now begun to be appreciated.

The main plus point is that you get a lot of house for your money. A thirties house in the suburbs costs about 40 per cent less than the same-sized Victorian house further into town. The quality of building was high in the 1930s, so you'll find that an unmodernized house from that time is in better structural condition than most period homes. The gardens are generous, often running right round the house, and there's usually off-street parking.

Furthermore, houses of this period are full of attractive features such as parquet flooring, big doors, wood panelling, detailed fireplaces and stained-glass windows. Room sizes are larger than in Victorian homes, the views often better and the layouts more adaptable. Prices are rising most rapidly in thirties estates that are near to town or city centres.

# New homes

The great plus point of buying a new home is that everything is brand spanking new, so (in theory, at least) you don't have to worry about things like dry rot and damp or boilers breaking down. If you are buying from the builder, you may also be given a choice of colours, carpets, fixtures and fittings, so there won't be any redecorating to do when you move in. Running costs should also be lower because new houses are better insulated than older ones.

Another advantage is their mortgageability. Sometimes the builder will offer you a 100 per cent mortgage (if so, be sure to compare their interest rate with that of other lenders). You won't need a full structural survey as new homes are guaranteed by the National House Building Council (NHBC) for ten years, and for the first two of those years any structural defects have to be put right by the builder free of charge.

On the down side, there's no escaping the fact that the majority of new homes are not as well built as houses that date from before the Second World War. They don't have as much character and the rooms tend to be smaller. Also, some new estates are situated rather far from shops, pubs and other amenities. Nevertheless, most modern private developments offer a good lifestyle, especially for families.

# Property types

The type of house you consider will depend not only on how much space you need, but also on what you can afford in your chosen area.

### Terraced

Terraced houses (apart from five-storey Regency jobs) tend to be cheaper than detached or semi-detached houses and are a good choice for first-time buyers. Few have garages so there may be a parking problem, and gardens or patios tend to be small. Find out how noisy the neighbours are before committing to a terraced house.

### Semi-detached

These are joined to another house on one side, so it only matters if the neighbours on that side are noisy. Semis are ideal for family life. Most have a garage and a garden.

### Detached

These aren't attached to any other dwelling and usually have big gardens. They are perfect for big families and rock guitarists. Noise from neighbours would only be a problem in the garden. Detached houses are generally more expensive than terraced houses or semis, but are a good investment.

## Bungalows

Bungalows abound in outer suburbs and seaside resorts. They are particularly sought after by retired people because there are no stairs to climb. They can be detached or semi-detached and are ideal for single people or couples with no children living at home. They usually have quite generous gardens.

## Flats

Flats are most common in towns, especially London, where they account for 28 per cent of all homes. Unless they're in very swanky developments, flats are cheaper than houses so they're the obvious choice for first-time buyers, whether singles or couples. A flat is called a 'conversion' if it's in a big old house that has been converted into flats, and 'purpose-built' if the building was originally designed as flats. Lots of people feel safer living in a flat, especially if it has a good entryphone system and is not on the ground floor. The other great advantage, if you have limited free time, is that there's no garden to keep up and usually no exterior maintenance to worry about.

Bear in mind that the legal fees connected with buying a flat may be higher than for a house, because there is more work involved in checking out the terms of the lease. Your solicitor has to be satisfied, on your behalf, that the right provision has been made for the maintenance of the building and that you won't be landed with unexpected bills.

## Freehold or leasehold

Although the basic difference between freehold and leasehold is easily understood, there can be complications with both kinds of tenure.

### Leasehold flats

Most flats are sold leasehold (on a long lease), which means you own it for the number of years on the lease and pay a small ground rent to the landlord. At the end of the lease the ownership of the flat reverts to the landlord, so the longer the lease the more valuable the property. Although anything over 21 years counts as a long lease, it is probably not worth considering a flat with less than 70 years to run on the lease, as you may have difficulty getting a mortgage and the property's value won't increase much unless you pay to extend the lease. This used to be difficult, but the new Commonhold and Leasehold Reform Act 2002 has made it much easier to obtain lease extensions and new longer leases (see the box on page 33).

Leasehold flat-owners normally pay an annual service charge for maintenance and communal services. The amount should be stated on the estate agent's particulars – if not, ask how much it is before viewing the property. This charge covers the upkeep of the building and grounds, and the cleaning of communal areas. Sometimes service charges don't include major repairs and redecoration, so do find out what happens when these are needed, as sudden extra charges can come as a shock. A great many flat-owners are deeply dissatisfied with the way their blocks are managed. Under the new legislation, they now have the right to take over the management of their buildings.

## Leasehold houses

Some houses are sold leasehold but this arrangement is simpler as, normally, the leaseholder alone is responsible for the maintenance of the building. The 2002 Commonhold and Leasehold Reform Act gives leaseholders of houses, who have previously extended their lease, the right to buy the freehold of their property or the right to an assured tenancy after the expiry of their extended lease.

Any long lease, whether for a flat or a house, needs careful scrutiny by an experienced solicitor.

## Freehold

Most houses are sold freehold, which means you are the outright owner of the property and the land it stands on. About a quarter of privately owned flats come with a share of the freehold. This means there is still a lease for each flat, but you and the other flat-owners in the building own the land on which the property stands and have the right to live there indefinitely. One main advantage is that the freeholders, acting as joint landlords, can grant themselves longer leases without having to pay a premium. They can also jointly agree to change any terms of the lease that are unsatisfactory.

As there's no outside landlord, you are jointly responsible for maintaining the exterior and common parts of the building. You can employ a managing agent to handle this or you can form a company, settle a maintenance charge between you and pay it into your joint bank account for use as and when needed. Shared freeholds are most common in converted houses that contain just three or four flats.

A few flats are completely freehold – each flat-owner owns their own flat outright, so there are no leases. Some lenders don't like this, even when there are only a couple of flats in the building, because there's no legal agreement (though there may be an informal one) about who will pay if there is subsidence or if the roof caves in. The only way round this is to find a lender who doesn't mind, or get a solicitor to draw up a shared freehold.

# The Commonhold and Leasehold Reform Act 2002

This Act created a new type of ownership. In the past, leasehold tenure (which is almost unique to England and Wales) has been heavily weighted in favour of landlords. However, the 1993 Leasehold Reform Act improved the situation by giving certain qualifying flat-owners the right to extend their leases, acquire new 90-year leases or buy their freeholds. The new 2002 Act has improved things still further by relaxing the qualifying rules.

Part 1 of the Act (due to be fully implemented in Spring 2004) introduces a new form of tenure for newly developed blocks of flats, called Commonhold. Under this system, owner-occupiers have absolute ownership of their own individual flats and share ownership of the communal parts, which they manage collectively. Commonhold is also available for existing buildings or developments where all the leaseholders agree to buy out whoever owns the freehold. The system is similar, in effect, to having a share of the freehold.

Part 2 of the Act helps flat-owners who can't or don't wish to convert to Commonhold. It:

- gives leaseholders the right to take over the management of their buildings
- allows anyone owning a long lease for at least two years to extend it
- strengthens leaseholders' rights regarding service charges
- makes it easier for leaseholders of flats to buy collectively the freehold of their building.

Most of Part 2 is already in force; the rest will be implemented in stages from Spring 2004.

## Extending a lease

The amount you pay to extend a lease depends on the extra value (called the 'marriage value') created when the lease has been extended, and on how much the landlord is losing by giving up some of his/her interest in the property. Obviously a flat with 40 years left on the lease becomes worth much more if the lease is extended to 90 years. In the past, leaseholders buying a lease extension had to pay the landlord at least 50 per cent of the extra value, as well as a premium for the additional years. Under the new Act, leaseholders buying an extended lease will not have to pay any marriage value if the unexpired term of the lease is 80 years or more. If it's less than 80 years, the amount due is 50 per cent of the marriage value, not *at least* 50 per cent.

The new Act has given leasehold home-owners important and much needed rights regarding the value and management of their homes.

# Tower blocks and ex-council property

In the 1960s, high-rise housing was considered a social ideal. As the slums (mainly the Victorian terraces we now love) were demolished, people queued up to move into the modern, 30-storey concrete blocks. But, for what should have been obvious reasons, the experiment failed. People felt cut off in their little boxes in the sky, children had nowhere to play and community spirit was lost.

But some tower blocks are getting a new lease of life. One, the 32-storey Trellick Tower in west London (once known as the 'tower of terror'), has become terrifically fashionable, with flats changing hands for £200,000. Residents rave about the views, the light and the sunsets and, because of its pioneering design, English Heritage has made it a listed building.

The difference is that the block is now well managed, with entryphones, faster, bigger lifts and 24-hour security with CCTV. This attracts a different kind of resident – busy career people who like the views and want a low-maintenance home in the heart of town.

In general, high-rise flats are still not seen as a good investment because they can be hard to resell. But more and more people are buying them and, if you choose your block carefully, they are a way to get a foot on the property ladder. Things to look out for include:

- a good area
- a good structure
- adequate security.

It is not always easy to get a mortgage on ex-council property, though houses and low-rise blocks are less problematic. Everything depends on the area, the construction of the building and how many other owner-occupiers there are. Some lenders, concerned about vandalism, will consider a high-rise flat only if it is between the fourth and seventh floors, while others will lend only if the block is no more than four storeys high. Some are concerned about buildings insurance since, if only some residents are owner-occupiers, there's no simple way of making sure that the whole building is properly insured.

Resale value is also an issue. Some people who bought under local authority 'right to buy' schemes have had problems selling their properties because there are very few other owner-occupiers on the estate. According to the Halifax, everything depends on their expert valuer's opinion about the state of the market in that precise location.

But they don't want to discourage first-time buyers from looking at ex-council flats because some are very good buys. Once again, it's all about location. Low-rise ex-council flats in newly fashionable areas such as Mortlake in south-west London fetch nearly the same prices as non-council flats.

### Existing council tenants

You have a right to buy your council house or flat at a considerable discount if you have lived in it as a secure tenant for more than two years. The amount of discount is normally between 40 and 70 per cent, depending on how long you have lived there. If you want to take advantage of this, do so quickly as the right-to-buy laws may soon change. But first think carefully about how easy the property will be to sell, and bear in mind that if you do sell in under three years any profit belongs to the council.

## Warehouse and dockland developments

The attractive dockland developments in many British towns and cities have proved one of the best investments of recent years – many dockland-dwellers have seen their properties double and even triple in value over the past ten years. It's not hard to understand why they're so popular: views over water, parking spaces, a choice of new homes from family town houses to loft-style apartments, all fitted out to a high standard and very handy for the town centre. Dockland warehouse conversions with their vast living rooms and wide windows are also much sought after.

But it's hard to find a waterside bargain these days, as most dockland developments have already up and come, and homes with a waterside view cost about 20 per cent more than those without.

But if warehouse living appeals, try looking elsewhere. There are still lots of nineteenth-century industrial buildings in city centres, some of which are being turned into mixed developments of homes, offices, shops and restaurants. In Manchester, Birmingham, Newcastle, Leeds and Glasgow, as well as many parts of London, interesting old buildings, from cotton mills to former department stores (many of which have stood empty for years), are being converted into flats and loft apartments, often with panoramic views and cafés or gyms on the ground floor.

While not ideal for families, these are perfect for singles, couples, first-time buyers and anyone else who wants large rooms and views just a stone's throw from the city centre. The only drawbacks are that parking can be difficult (unless there's an underground car park), management charges may be high, and you could be surrounded by an unattractive building site for the first few years.

But warehouse conversions are a good investment, and you'll have the added satisfaction of knowing that, by moving into an environmentally friendly 'brownfield' development (new homes on recycled building land), you're doing your bit to encourage inner-city regeneration and protect the countryside from being built on.

## A complete wreck

If you can stand the hassle, the best way to end up with a property worth far more than you paid for it is to buy a wreck and renovate it yourself, with the help of some experienced and reliable builders. Remember that you'll need somewhere to live while the work is going on.

The days are long gone when lovely old agricultural buildings and run-down, once-elegant town houses could be picked up for a song, though there are still some bargains to be had in remote rural areas. Estate agents usually have one or two ruins on their books, or you could try an auction house. Unfortunately, property developers often get there first, especially in towns. They can outbid private buyers because their renovation costs are lower as they use their own builders. There's more about doing up a wreck in Chapter 7.

## Self-build

If you can't afford, or are fed up with trying to find, the kind of house you really want, one way to acquire the home of your dreams – and pay around 30 per cent less for it than you would on the open market – is to build it yourself. You don't literally build it yourself (unless you want to): you find a plot of land with building permission (about quarter of an acre is a reasonable size for a house and garden) and then get the house of your choice put up on it. Most self-builders go for a one-off, architect-designed brick and block house, but a substantial proportion (around 25 per cent) choose 'ready-made' timber-frame designs from specialist companies, which can be adapted to individual needs. These houses are still built up from scratch (not prefabricated), but the timber frame and panels are made-to-measure in a factory.

The hardest part is finding a plot, especially in the South East where land is scarce and expensive. You also have to get a special self-build mortgage, which is released in instalments as you tackle each stage. The average cost of a self-build house, including the plot, is around £192,000, but this varies enormously from county to county. A four-bedroom house will cost £71,000–100,000 to build, but in Oxfordshire, for example, just a plot costs as much as £250,000. The company Buildstore specializes in self-build projects and there's lots of information on their website: www.buildstore.co.uk

Self-build is not a project for the faint-hearted – you may have to live in a caravan on the site while your house is being built – but it is becoming increasingly popular. One in every four new detached houses is self-built and the number of self-build homes completed each year has risen from around 2,000 in 1978 to more than 20,000 today. According to the Joseph Rowntree Foundation (*Homes to DIY For – The UK's self-build market in the 21st century*), with greater use of new building technologies and certain changes to land provision and planning policy, self-build could grow to around 10 per cent of the new-private-homes market.

## SELF-BUILD — CASE STUDY

**Having realized that they could have a much better home if they built it themselves, John and Sue B bought a plot of land in a small Worcestershire village in 2000, about 18 months before they got married.** The plot cost £40,000 and came with detailed planning permission. They chose a timber-frame kit for their house after seeing one at a self-build exhibition at Birmingham's National Exhibition Centre. The frame itself was erected by the suppliers, and John and Sue then used local subcontractors to build the rest of the house. Being a practical chap, John was able to organize the builders and tradesmen and do some of the work himself. As he was using a trade account and mortgage arranged by a specialist self-build company, he also had access to free advice from their local consultant.

The four-bedroom house started to go up in April, and by the time John and Sue got married in November it was ready to move into, at a building cost of around £100,000. They're now hard at work landscaping the garden – and the house has been valued at £240,000.

### Self-build co-operatives

This is similar to the self-build scheme described above, but it involves actual DIY building. A number of families purchase a piece of land that is big enough to hold a house for each family, and then help to build each others' houses, sharing labour and costs. Quite a lot of money can be saved, but this is a long-term commitment with numerous terms and conditions. It is usually done under the guidance of a company that specializes in self-build schemes.

# A place in the sun

Countless people get the urge to leave grey skies behind for ever when they retire, Spain being the most popular choice for Britons. As with moving from town to country, it makes sense to rent rather than buy (and to let your UK home, rather than selling it) before committing yourself. Ideally, keep your British property anyway, in case you have to return.

Property prices abroad may seem cheap, but don't forget that there will be additional costs like medical insurance and visits back to the UK, on top of living expenses (and exchange rates can fluctuate). Now that quarantine rules have changed there's no problem with pets, but how much are you going to miss friends and family?

Other considerations:

- Don't go into 'holiday mode' when house-hunting abroad. Treat the purchase as rigorously as you would at home
- The best deals are on older, inland properties
- Don't be pressurized by anyone, and be wary of companies offering their buying services who want to pick you up at the airport
- There are big differences between UK law and the law in other countries – in Spain, for example, contracts to purchase property can become binding very quickly. Get translations of all documents, and take legal advice before signing anything
- When choosing a property, check that no new developments will spoil your view or your peace
- If the property is part of a community development, how much are the community fees? Do the fees include connection to gas, water and electricity?
- Is the property near all the amenities you need?
- Arrange your own survey to identify structural problems
- In some countries, including Spain, debts can be attached to a property so get a lawyer to check whether this applies to the one you're interested in
- Allow 10 per cent of the purchase price for local taxes and legal fees.
- You will need to learn the language – without it you could feel lost and isolated
- Your application for permanent residence in a country may not include the right to work
- If you are taking your own furniture, remember that UK electrical appliances may be unusable abroad
- You may be liable to pay tax in your adopted country – seek professional advice.

# Retirement homes

Many developers now sell sheltered housing for older people. This may be a new development of flats and cottages, or converted flats in large country houses. Some are freehold, others are leasehold, with a service charge for the cleaning and maintenance of communal areas. Many developments have laundry rooms, lounges, dining rooms, guest suites and sometimes even gyms and swimming pools. There is usually a resident manager and the homes are equipped with alarm buttons.

Although most of these developments are in suburbs, villages or small country towns, more and more are springing up in places like Chelsea and Bath, because the old idea of retiring to a quiet country place with roses round the door no longer appeals to the new breed of sprightlier older person. Now that they have the freedom to do as they please, they want to be near bright lights, sophistication and culture.

If you are thinking of buying a retirement home, here are a few points to consider:

- What facilities does the development have for residents?
- Can you park your car?
- Is the development near transport and shops?
- Do the builder and management have experience of providing retirement housing?
- Is the management a member of the Association of Retirement Housing Managers?
- What is included in the service charge – does it include a 'sinking fund' for repairs?
- Will you get the full market value of your home back if you resell?
- What happens if your health deteriorates?

# Ownership trends

**In recent years there has been a fundamental shift in housing demand, due to the growth in the number of single people buying properties.** In 2002, according to the Halifax, single buyers accounted for more than 40 per cent of buyers, compared with only 25 per cent in 1983. The fastest growing group of home-owners in Britain is single women, who now account for 17 per cent of all home-buyers (compared with 8 per cent in 1983). In the days when the vast majority of buyers were couples, the demand was for terraced and semi-detached houses, but today's young singles are looking for flats or maisonettes. Unfortunately, there aren't enough affordable ones, particularly in London and the South East, which is why the number of first-time buyers in these areas is dwindling.

Flats are in demand not only because they suit single people's needs but also because they are usually cheaper than houses. Ideally, in high-priced areas like London, there should be many more studio flats on the market – good-sized rooms with areas for sleeping, living and cooking, plenty of storage space and a separate bathroom. Many first-time buyers are kept out of the market because there aren't any studios and they can't afford two-room properties.

There are a number of alternative routes to owning property: sharing with friends, buying alone and letting a room, or going through a housing association.

## Buying with friends

Pooling resources with one or more friends will give you a bigger deposit and a bigger mortgage loan. Banks and building societies don't mind if you are borrowing with a friend rather than a partner as long as you fulfil their normal lending criteria. They usually lend first-time buyers up to three or sometimes four times their salary. Joint first-time buyers will get three times one salary plus the second, or 2.5 times the joint salary. If three or four people want to buy together, that's possible too. Some lenders will only take two salaries into consideration for lending purposes (although all three or four names can be put on the mortgage and the title deeds), but others will allow three times three salaries or 2.75 times the income of four friends, as long as they are not borrowing more than 75 per cent of the value of the property. The multiples will be lower if you are borrowing 75–95 per cent.

The crucial thing to remember is that everyone named on the mortgage is 'jointly and severally' responsible for paying the debt. This means that if one joint owner stops paying their agreed share of the mortgage, the lender will expect the others named on the mortgage to make up the difference. In other words, if your mates renege on the agreement you are lumbered.

When buying with someone else, you have to decide whether you will be joint tenants or tenants in common.

### Joint tenants

With a joint tenancy agreement, you both own equal shares in the property and if one dies the other automatically inherits their share. Married couples and long-term partners, especially if they have children, usually opt for joint tenancy.

### Tenants in common

Tenants in common can own equal or unequal shares in the property, and each owner is free to dispose of their share in any way they wish. This is most sensible when friends are buying together.

## Buy on your own and let a room

There's not much point in getting the maximum possible mortgage loan if you are then so strapped for cash that you have to stay in and watch telly every night (or the goldfish if you can't afford a TV set). One way round this is to buy a place with a second bedroom and let the extra room to a friend or lodger whose rent will help pay your mortgage. Two-bedroom flats don't cost twice as much as one-bedroom ones, so the extra rent money should easily cover the higher mortgage payments.

Obliging parents come in useful here – if they are prepared to guarantee your mortgage payments, you may be able to borrow a bit more than your salary alone would allow. But they would have to prove that, if push came to shove, they could pay your mortgage for you, or at least the part of it that they have guaranteed.

## Housing associations

Some people manage to get a foot on the property ladder with the help of a housing association 'shared ownership' scheme. These schemes were introduced to help people who can't afford to buy a home outright but who have a few thousand pounds in savings and earn enough for a mortgage of, say, £50,000–£80,000.

The way it works is that you (or you and a friend/friends) buy a share of the property and pay a low rent on the remaining share you don't own. You can gradually buy further shares until eventually you own your home outright. The price of these further shares is based on the current value of the property, so if house prices go up over time, you will have to pay more for the same percentage.

Most people start off with a 50 per cent share, though you can buy as little as 25 per cent or as much as 75 per cent. The more of the property you own, the less rent you pay.

Shared ownership schemes are funded by the Housing Corporation through the Social Housing Grant and are run by housing associations and other registered social landlords. Applicants must be first-time buyers, and priority is given to people who are existing public sector tenants, or on local authority or social landlords' waiting lists.

Adults who still live at home with parents/relatives or have to leave rented accommodation are eligible, as long as they have some savings, a steady job, can raise a mortgage and have never owned a property. So if that describes your current situation and the idea appeals, put your name on your local authority housing register and express an interest in shared ownership. They will pass your name to the housing associations who operate in your area.

It's also worth filling in the individual housing associations' application forms. The Housing Corporation website (www.housingcorp.gov.uk) will tell you which ones work with your local housing department. Normally you can only apply through the housing department of the local authority for the area where you currently live.

Most of the homes that come up are already owned or part-owned by the housing associations, though some schemes allow you to choose a home on the open market. There are always waiting lists, but there's also a constant turnover. Quite a few schemes are aimed exclusively at 'key' workers, so you'll stand a better chance if you are, for example, a teacher, a health worker or in the police.

Under another scheme called Homebuy (open only to existing council or housing association tenants or those in housing need) you can get an interest-free loan of 25 per cent of the value of a home that is for sale on the open market. You finance the other 75 per cent with a normal mortgage on which you do, of course, pay interest. When you come to sell the property you have to repay the social landlord 25 per cent of its current value. One of the objects of this scheme is to free up rented accommodation for those on council waiting lists.

## What next?

Once you've decided on the sort of property you want to buy, it's time to investigate a mortgage. Having this theoretically in place before you start flat or house-hunting will enable you to move much more quickly when you find that ideal home.

Mortgage Loan
Agreement

er) are:

# 3

# All about mortgages

**Few people have the means to buy a property outright with their own savings or capital; most of us need to take out a mortgage – a long-term loan secured against the property.** This means that you can't sell the property without repaying the mortgage and, if you fail to keep up the payments, the lender (or 'mortgagee') has the right to repossess or claim the house/flat back from you – the 'mortgagor'. If you can pay the whole price of a property, then you're in an enviable position because everyone prefers a cash buyer and you are far more likely to get a daringly low offer accepted.

But the next best thing to not needing a mortgage is to have one agreed in principle before you find your property. It will enable you to proceed more quickly and so reduce the risk of being gazumped. Bear in mind that most 'in principle' mortgage offers are valid for only six months.

# Mortgage basics

There are a lot of different mortgage deals out there and it's worth shopping around for a good one *before* you start to look for the home of your dreams.

## Where to get a mortgage

Mortgages can be obtained from:

- building societies
- banks
- specialist or centralized lenders.

### Building societies

These are owned by and for their members and have been the traditional source of mortgages for more than a century. There are about 60 societies in the UK, some with hundreds of branches, others with just a few. Local building societies offer some of the best rates around and will often lend on properties outside their own area. As mutual societies, they aim to offer lower interest rates than other lenders.

### Banks

High street banks came into the mortgage market relatively recently. They offer a full range of products, but tend to prefer customers who can put down deposits of 10 per cent or more. Several former building societies, such as the Halifax and the Woolwich, are now banks.

### Specialist or centralized lenders

These tend to specialize in non-standard mortgages, lending to the self-employed, people with poor credit histories or borrowers who are buying properties to rent out. Some of the big banks have their own subsidiaries that specialize in this section of the market. Many specialist mortgage lenders encourage you to apply by phone or over the Internet.

## How mortgages work

Because a mortgage is secured against a property, the interest rates are lower than with a normal bank loan. Mortgages are repaid over the course of a fixed term (usually twenty-five years) or at the end of a fixed term, and interest is charged on the outstanding amount (the amount you still owe) throughout that time. Interest rates go up and down according to the state of the economy, and they make a huge difference to your monthly outgoings.

Imagine you have a new £80,000 mortgage. If variable interest rates remain at around 4.5 per cent you will pay £3,600 a year or £300 a month purely in interest. On top of that there would be capital repayments (or payments into an investment scheme designed to pay off the mortgage at the end of the term). If interest rates went up to 9 per cent, you would find yourself paying £7,200 a year, or £600 a month in interest. You may think it unlikely that mortgage rates would double, but as recently as 2001 standard variable rates stood at around 7 per cent, and it's a sobering thought that in 1991/2 the average building society mortgage interest rate rose to 14.9 per cent. With an £80,000 loan, that would mean paying £11,920 a year, or £993 a month purely in interest. It's not surprising there were so many repossessions.

No one is predicting that kind of rise in the near future, but it does make sense to work out what size of mortgage you could afford if interest rates were to rise, say, by 2 or 3 per cent (as recently as 1997, the average rate was 6.8 per cent). The following table shows how monthly payments on a normal repayment mortgage, over a 25-year term, rise with stepped-up interest rates.

| Monthly payments (£s) over 25 years with increased interest rates | | | | | | |
|---|---|---|---|---|---|---|
| Loan | 3.5% | 4.0% | 4.5% | 5% | 5.5% | 6% |
| 50,000 | 250.31 | 263.91 | 277.91 | 292.29 | 307.04 | 322.15 |
| 75,000 | 375.46 | 395.86 | 416.87 | 438.44 | 460.56 | 483.22 |
| 100,000 | 500.63 | 527.83 | 555.83 | 584.59 | 614.08 | 644.30 |
| 150,000 | 750.93 | 791.75 | 833.74 | 876.88 | 921.13 | 966.45 |

*Source:* Halifax

Over a typical 25-year mortgage period, the total cost of your mortgage will be between two and three times the original home loan, which may be a sobering thought. On the bright side, the value of your property is likely to rise a great deal more than that in the same timespan. And you only really need to work out what a mortgage will cost you over 25 years if you are going to stay with that property and that mortgage for all that time. Most people move on from both.

# How much can you afford to borrow?

**The range of UK mortgages has increased dramatically in the past few years – there are now more than 250 lenders offering thousands of different permutations.** But the fact that borrowing to buy a property has become relatively easy doesn't mean that keeping up the repayments will be easy, too. Even if a lender is prepared to advance you a large amount (and the sky is more or less the limit if you are prepared to pay the higher interest rates that go with a self-certified or no-proof-of-income mortgage), it's essential to make sure you can afford the repayments – not only now but if interest rates were to double.

Mortgage lenders do their best to make sure that you are able to keep up the repayments, but of course they don't know anything about your real lifestyle. So before committing yourself to an enormous mortgage, it's a good idea to list all your monthly outgoings. For example:

- mortgage payments _____
- council tax _____
- loan payments _____
- credit card payments _____
- service charges and ground rent (if you're buying a leasehold property) _____
- insurance _____
- gas/electricity/phone _____
- travel/car expenses _____

- childcare/education _____
- food/eating out/pubs _____
- clothing _____
- hairdressing/beauty _____
- films/concerts/outings _____
- home entertainment _____
- gym/sports _____

**Total** _____

Deduct the total from your after-tax income and, hopefully, you will find you can manage easily. If not, then you should get a smaller mortgage – or rethink your lifestyle. Most people's mortgages account for between 15 and 25 per cent of their income, but there's no 'right' proportion because it all depends on the size of your income, your priorities and how much you spend on other things. Don't forget to budget for all the extra expenses when you first move to your new home.

# How much will they lend you?

**Up to 3.5 times your gross income if you're buying alone, or 2.5 times a couple's joint income.** But it's worth shopping around because there are so many permutations. Some lenders will allow you to borrow up to four times your gross income if you're buying alone, and 2.75 times two salaries. Others offer three to four times one salary plus the second salary.

You can work out how much you can afford to pay for a home by adding whatever cash you have for a deposit to the amount you will be allowed to borrow. Remember that you will need some of the cash to cover things like surveys, stamp duty and conveyancing (see the table on page 20).

Most lenders have the same basic rules, which are that you should:

- be in a steady job
- be able to prove your income
- have a good credit record
- provide a landlord's reference if you are a first-time buyer.

Interest rates tend to be lower, and more special deals are available, if you are not seeking a high Loan To Value (LTV). LTV is the percentage of the purchase price that the mortgage loan accounts for. To qualify for the cheapest home loans, you generally need to have a deposit of around 25 per cent of the purchase price.

## Options for self-employed borrowers and others

The self-employed, contract workers and people with more than one job are all bundled together with credit-impaired borrowers as problem or 'sub-prime' applicants. This means they are penalized with higher interest rates, which seems absurd when there are now around 3.2 million self-employed people in the UK.

Self-employed borrowers usually have to produce two to three years of audited accounts. The problem here is that your friendly accountant will, quite rightly, have minimized your tax liability. This is fine for income tax, but when it comes to applying for a mortgage it can make you seem less profitable and so less attractive to a mortgage lender. Some lenders only offer loans to self-employed people if their turnover shows an increase every year, while others take an average of their income over the last three years and offer three times that.

There are always lenders who are happy to take you on – at a price – whatever your circumstances, but there's no escaping the fact that it is harder to get a good mortgage deal if you are not a salaried nine-to-fiver.

## Self-certification

If you can't or would rather not produce three years' accounts, you can opt for a self-certified mortgage. This allows you to certify your own income by signing a document stating how much you earn, and is ideal for new businesses. First-time buyers are likely to be asked to supply a landlord's reference, and existing home-owners will have to produce recent mortgage statements.

Some lenders (such as Birmingham Midshires, Bristol and West, UCB Home Loans and Mortgage Express) cater specially for self-certification, and it makes sense to deal with them as they are more likely than mainstream lenders to judge an application on its own merits.

All lenders are likely to require:

- another lender's reference
- a credit search
- a solicitor's confirmation of previous home-ownership
- tax assessments
- landlord's reference.

A self-certified mortgage does have disadvantages:

- You may only be offered 3.25 times your stated income
- You will not get more than 85 per cent (sometimes 75 per cent) of the property's value
- The interest rate will be higher than for a mortgage based on proven income.

Allegations have been made in the media that applicants for self-certification mortgages have been encouraged by advisers to exaggerate their salaries in order to get a mortgage for that dream home. This may result in lenders reviewing their procedures, so do check before you consider this option. And remember, it is illegal to make a false statement about your income.

## Full-status mortgage

These are designed for 'sub-prime' applicants – people with less than perfect credit records – and are mainly offered by specialist lenders. This is more or less the only type of mortgage available to applicants with county court judgements for debt (CCJs) or who have had a home repossessed or a business go bankrupt. Some mainstream lenders are also dubious about people who have fallen behind on credit-card or hire-purchase payments.

The terms of a full-status mortgage are that you tell the lender everything about your circumstances and it makes its offer on that basis. Interest rates will be higher than with other mortgages, but they should go down once you have established a good payment record and proved you are a reliable borrower. If they don't, you can take your improved financial status to another lender.

## 100 per cent mortgages

Normally you are expected to have at least a 5 per cent deposit to put towards the purchase of your home, and your mortgage would pay for the other 95 per cent. In lenders' parlance, this is a 95 per cent LTV.

However, quite a few lenders are willing to offer a 100 per cent mortgage, providing your income can support this. Interest rates will be higher, though, and you may have to pay for an insurance policy called a Mortgage Indemnity Guarantee (MIG). Some lenders insist on this for any LTV over 90 per cent.

Although you pay for the MIG, it only protects the lender, who will be able to recoup the outstanding amount of the loan if the property has to be repossessed and sold for less than the amount of the mortgage. The premium is charged on a sliding scale and is paid on the proportion of the loan above 75 per cent – so if you are buying a property for £100,000 it is paid on £25,000. With a 100 per cent mortgage, the MIG may cost 10 per cent of this sum, so you will pay a £2,500 insurance premium. Some lenders disguise the MIG by calling it a 'high lending fee'.

To soften the blow, you may be allowed to add the MIG premium to your mortgage loan, but then of course you will be paying interest on it for 25 years. Alternatively, you can sometimes opt to pay it in 36 instalments. Either way, an MIG is something to be avoided, so try to find a lender who doesn't demand it.

# Types of mortgage

**There are just two basic types of mortgage – repayment, or interest-only linked to an investment scheme.** But, as we shall see there are countless different deals within these categories.

## Repayment mortgage

With a repayment mortgage, you pay monthly interest on the loan plus a repayment instalment. In the early years your interest payments are much bigger than your capital repayments but the balance changes over time. Repayment mortgages are simple and have many advantages:

- The loan will definitely be paid off at the end of the mortgage term
- The size of the loan is being constantly reduced, so negative equity is less likely to be a problem
- When you sell the property, any equity you have built up (after repaying the loan) can be put towards your next home
- There's no need for a linked insurance or savings plan (though if you have dependants it's important to take out a separate life insurance policy)
- Your investment is not dependent on the stock market
- It reduces the impact of potential higher interest rates, especially in the later years of the mortgage, because the capital has been reduced.

## Interest-only mortgage

With an interest-only mortgage, your monthly payments to the mortgage lender consist of interest only. As you are not paying off the loan itself, you also need a separate long-term investment plan that will grow enough funds to pay off the loan at the end of the repayment period. This can be an ISA (Individual Savings Account), an endowment or a pension scheme.

Such plans are slightly cheaper than repayment mortgages and hold out all sorts of promises, such as early repayment of the mortgage or a substantial lump sum to enjoy at the end of the mortgage term, but neither is guaranteed – in fact, the plan may not even succeed in paying off your loan. Interest-only mortgages with investment plans are not very useful if you are likely to move house a lot, as what you really want in these circumstances is to pay off as much of your loan as you can and build up some equity to invest in your next home.

Some lenders allow you to divide your mortgage so that part of it is a repayment scheme and part is run on an interest-only basis.

## ISA mortgage

ISAs replaced Personal Equity Plans (PEPs) in 1999/2000. This form of investment is tax-free, so if your plan performs well you just might have a nice nest egg left over after the mortgage has been repaid at the end of the term. Or you may be able to pay off the loan early. Some 'packaged' ISA mortgages include built-in life or term assurance. If not, you should arrange this separately.

The advantages of an ISA mortgage:

- It's tax-efficient
- It provides a possible surplus lump sum
- It provides for the possible early repayment of the loan.

The disadvantages:

- There is no guarantee the loan will be repaid
- Tax-free benefits are not guaranteed as legislation could change
- Your debt remains the same throughout the mortgage period.

## Pension mortgage

This, too, is an interest-only mortgage, but the additional investment plan takes the form of a personal pension – a stock-market-based investment that, because it is a pension, benefits from tax relief and tax-free growth. At the end of the term, 25 per cent of the plan's value is used to pay off your mortgage; the rest goes to provide a retirement income.

You can't use more than 25 per cent to cover your mortgage, because the other 75 per cent must by law be used to buy a pension. Pension mortgages are popular mainly with the self-employed because they combine buying a home with saving for the future, and the investment can be taken from property to property.

The advantages of a pension mortgage:

- It is extremely tax-efficient, especially for higher rate tax-payers
- It has built-in life cover
- You can contribute additional lump sums.

The disadvantages:

- The debt remains constant
- You can't get at the money until you are 50
- The lump sum can't be used for other purposes
- The tax situation regarding pensions may change
- There is no guarantee that you will have accumulated enough to pay off the mortgage at the end of the period, as the fund could underperform.

## Endowment mortgage

Endowment mortgages have recently acquired a bad name because a sizeable proportion of people who took them out some years ago have been warned that, due to underperforming investments, the final lump sum won't be enough to pay off their mortgage – despite the fact that when they were sold the product they were told that it definitely would. Those who can prove they were mis-sold endowment policies can seek financial compensation.

With an endowment mortgage, you make two monthly payments: one is an interest payment to your mortgage lender, the other you invest with an insurance company in an endowment policy. This policy is designed to grow throughout the mortgage term into a substantial lump sum that will pay off your loan – and hopefully provide an extra lump sum. However, everything depends on the fund's performance – you might make some extra money or be left with a shortfall.

There are two types of endowment policy: with-profits and unit-linked. A with-profits policy pools your monthly premiums with the funds of all the other investors. Depending on the investment performance, it awards annual bonuses that cannot be taken away. However, a large proportion of the all-important final pay-out is in the form of a terminal bonus which is not guaranteed.

With a unit-linked policy, your premiums buy specific units in stock market investment. Unit-linked funds have the potential for greater growth than a with-profits endowment, but there is also a greater risk that they will perform badly.

The advantages of an endowment mortgage:
- There's the theoretical possibility that you will be able to pay off your mortgage early or receive a lump sum at the end of the repayment period
- You can transfer the mortgage to another property.

The disadvantages:
- It has high charges
- There is no guarantee that you will be able to pay off your mortgage
- If you cash it in early you are unlikely to get your money back.

## Interest-only with no investment plan

Sometimes, when there is no risk of negative equity (for example, if you are borrowing relatively little or when prices are rising very fast), it's possible to take out an interest-only mortgage with no investment plan, or with only life insurance. The idea is that the loan is paid off when the property is sold. This scheme makes good sense if you regard it as a short-term mortgage – for instance, if you are not planning to stay long in a property or are doing it up to sell. But it's unwise if you intend to spend many years there, as your loan will never decrease and you will eventually have to sell your home to pay it off.

# Interest

**The mortgage market has become more competitive in recent years, resulting in a bewildering array of approaches to charging interest.** But, basically, you still have two main choices – a variable rate or a fixed rate – although there are ways of combining the two, so part of your loan is fixed rate and the rest variable.

## Variable-rate mortgages

If you choose a variable-rate mortgage, your payments will go up or down according to what interest rates are doing generally.

### Standard variable-rate mortgages

The basic no-frills mortgage, these are still chosen by the majority of home-owners. Standard variable rates are based on the Bank of England's base rate, which means they move up and down as the base rate moves up and down. Rates vary from lender to lender but are typically 1.5 to 4 per cent above the base rate. Borrowers who have opted for a standard variable-rate mortgage do well when rates fall, but badly when rates rise. In order to avoid too-frequent adjustments to payments, most lenders work out the average standard rate over the past year and charge that for the whole of the following year. At the end of that year the interest is recalculated and payments are reset.

The advantages of a standard variable-rate mortgage:
- When the Bank of England's base rates fall, your payments go down as well
- You can move to another lender at any time without paying a penalty.

The disadvantages:
- If base rates rise sharply, so will your monthly payments
- Fluctuations in interest rates make it less easy to budget.

### Discount mortgages

These are standard variable-rate mortgages with a percentage deducted from the variable rate for a fixed period – from six months to several years. As the lender's standard variable rate moves up and down, so does the discount rate.

The advantages of a discount mortgage:
- It is helpful to have reduced payments during the first few years when you are spending money on things like furniture and carpets
- You benefit from any fall in the Bank of England's base rate.

The disadvantages:

- Beware of early redemption penalties, which often extend beyond the end of the discounted period. You may have to pay the equivalent of six months' mortgage repayments for moving during the penalty period
- When the discount period ends, you may be trapped in an uncompetitive rate of interest
- Your mortgage payments will suddenly increase when they revert to standard variable rate.

### Base-rate trackers (or tracker mortgages)

These are similar to standard variable rates, but because they are linked to – or 'track' – the bank base rate, any rise or fall in that rate is immediately followed by an equivalent rise or fall in your mortgage rate. Typically set at between 0.75 per cent and 1 per cent above base rate, tracker interest rates tend to be lower than standard variable rates.

Base-rate trackers are available for the full term of the mortgage or for a fixed term of, say, five years. They can also be combined with a discount offer. For example, you may be offered 0.5 per cent for the first two years, rising to 0.75 per cent after that.

The advantages of a base-rate tracker mortgage:

- The interest rate is usually lower than the lender's standard variable rate
- You benefit from all base rate drops, whereas these are not automatically passed on with standard variable-rate mortgages.

The disadvantages:

- There are early redemption penalties
- There is the possibility of sudden increases.

### Capped-rate mortgages

Here, too, the rate is variable, but you have a guarantee that it will not go above a set level – the cap. While it is under the cap, it goes up and down the same way as a standard variable rate. Capped-rate mortgages can sometimes be combined with discount mortgages.

The advantage of a capped-rate mortgage:

- You get the best of both worlds, in that your payments can go down, but cannot go up above a certain amount.

The disadvantages:

- Early redemption fees can extend beyond the capped period
- There is normally an application fee.

## Fixed-rate mortgages

A fixed-rate mortgage is just that – your payments will not go up or down for the length of the fixed-rate period, which can be anything from 6 months to 25 years. Long-term fixed rates tend to be 50 per cent higher than variable rates, and penalty clauses usually apply for the whole term. But you won't find many lenders offering long-term fixed-rate deals while interest rates are at rock bottom.

Two to five years is a typical fixed-rate period, and after that the interest rate reverts to the lender's standard variable rate. However, in his April 2003 Budget speech, the Chancellor said the government was looking at ways of encouraging long-term fixed-rate mortgages, as this would help to ensure the stability of the housing market.

All fixed-rate mortgages are a gamble in that both you and the lender are betting on what interest rates will do over that time. The lender is hoping they will fall, so they will make more money. You are hoping they will rise, so you can save money.

The advantages of a fixed-rate mortgage:

- It's easier to budget because you know exactly how much your mortgage repayments will be for a given period
- You are protected from any sudden increases in the base rate.

The disadvantages:

- There are early redemption penalties
- You may miss out on a drop in variable interest rates
- There's normally an arrangement fee.

## Cashback mortgages

It sounds almost too good to be true – after you have taken out your mortgage, the lender gives you back a lump sum (anything from £200 to 6 per cent or even 10 per cent of the loan) that you can use for whatever you like. Cashbacks are designed to attract borrowers who need some cash to help with their moving costs, and can also provide useful savings to fall back on in the first year or two of your mortgage.

But of course you are not really being given free cash. If the cashback is linked to a discount or fixed-rate mortgage, the interest rate will be higher than if there were no cashback. And there will be early redemption penalties. If you change lenders within five years you may have to repay the whole value of the cashback, or six months' mortgage payments. Cashbacks are available on both fixed- and variable-rate mortgages.

## CAT-standard mortgages

A CAT-standard mortgage is one that meets certain government-defined standards relating to Charges, Access and Terms. These standards are voluntary, so mortgage lenders don't have to use them and they don't apply to all mortgages. The information you get about a mortgage will normally say whether it's CAT-standard or not.

The advantage of a CAT-standard mortgage is that you can be confident that there are no nasty surprises lurking in the small print and that the terms won't suddenly change for the worse. But mortgages that are not CAT-standard are not necessarily bad buys. They may offer interesting or attractive features such as cashback or low interest rates, but be accompanied by charges or penalties that don't meet the CAT-standards.

But the fact that a mortgage is CAT-standard does not mean that it is guaranteed, recommended or endorsed by the government, or that is it the most suitable mortgage for you.

To sum up CAT-standards for mortgages:

### Charges
- Interest must be calculated daily.
- There is no separate charge for a mortgage indemnity guarantee (MIG).
- Full credit is given for all payments when they are made.
- Borrowers pay no fees to brokers.

### Variable-rate loans
- There is no arrangement fee.
- The interest rate is set at no more than 2 per cent above the Bank of England's base rate.
- When the base rate falls, the interest must be adjusted within a calendar month.
- No redemption charges apply at any time.

### Fixed- and capped-rate loans
- The maximum booking fee is £150.
- The maximum redemption charge is 1 per cent of the amount you owe for each remaining year of the fixed period, reducing monthly.
- There is no redemption charge after the end of the fixed or capped period.
- There is no redemption charge if you stay with the same mortgage lender when you move home.

## Access

- If there is a minimum amount you must borrow to get a CAT-standard mortgage, it must be £10,000 or less.
- Any customer may apply.
- The lender's normal lending criteria apply.
- You can continue with your CAT-standard mortgage when you move home, provided your lender is happy to lend on the new property.
- If you make regular payments, you can choose which day of the month to pay.
- You can make early repayments at any time.

## Terms

- All advertising and paperwork must be straightforward and clear.
- You do not have to buy any other products to get a CAT-standard mortgage.
- Your lender must give at least six months' notice if they can no longer offer your mortgage on CAT-standard terms.
- If you are in arrears you should pay the interest only on the outstanding debt at the normal rate.

# Mortgage brokers

**Mortgage brokers are the middlemen who bring you and your lender together – assuming you haven't approached a lender directly.** Some deal only with mortgages, while others are estate agents, accountants, financial advisers, insurance brokers or solicitors. The important thing is that they should be independent (not linked to any one insurance company or lender) and have access to a wide range of lenders. If they are not independent, they must tell you.

Banks and building society mortgage advisers only tell you about their own mortgage products. The advantage of a good independent broker – especially now there are so many different deals – is that they can help you choose a lender and a package that is right for your particular circumstances. They are especially useful if either you or the property is an unusual proposition. In some cases you have to pay them an arrangement fee – make sure this is not payable if for any reason you don't go ahead with the mortgage.

Bear in mind that even when a broker or financial adviser is independent, they get more commission from some products than others (especially if these are insurance or stock-market linked) and so may not always spell out the downside or be entirely unbiased in their advice. Always do your own homework to ensure that a recommended mortgage is really what you need.

## The Mortgage Code
The Council of Mortgage Lenders has developed a mortgage code, which lays down minimum standards which all mortgage lenders and intermediaries have to meet. The code sets out:
- how your mortgage should be arranged
- what information you should receive before you commit yourself
- how your mortgage should be dealt with once it is in place.

As a potential mortgage customer, you should be given a copy of the leaflet *You and Your Mortgage* at your first meeting to discuss a mortgage. This leaflet is published on the Mortgage Code Compliance Board website: www.mortgagecode.org.uk

Some 150 lenders and 13,000 intermediaries subscribe to the code. You can check whether a particular intermediary is a member by ringing the Mortgage Code Register of Intermediaries helpline on 01782 216 300.

A main aim of the code is to ensure that the mortgage sales process is as clear and transparent as possible. Anyone arranging a mortgage for a customer must ensure that information is provided on a range of aspects, including fees and charges, insurance, penalties for early repayment or defaulting on payments, and future repayments at the end of a fixed or discounted period.

Eight key questions to ask your mortgage lender or adviser:

1. What are my interest rate options (i.e. variable, fixed, capped, discounted)?
2. What will my monthly payments be? Get quotes on various different deals, and ask what you would be paying if interest rates doubled
3. Are there any redemption penalties for a fixed, capped or discounted deal? If so, how long do they run for?
4. How will my payments change at the end of a fixed, capped or discounted period? Do I have to go on to the standard variable rate, or are there other special deals?
5. Are there any special offers? Some lenders offer a free valuation or pay your legal fees, especially if you are a first-time buyer
6. What are the costs? Is there an application fee or arrangement fee and will I have to pay a Mortgage Indemnity Guarantee (MIG) premium?
7. Are there any conditions attached to the deal, like having to buy the lender's buildings, contents or life insurance?
8. Is it a flexible mortgage that will allow me to overpay, underpay and take payment holidays?

# New ways of managing your mortgage

**Mortgage lenders are always thinking up bright new ideas to attract new borrowers.** Some of these ideas, such as current-account mortgages (CAMs), have limited appeal. Who wants to be reminded that they are £150,000 in debt every time they read a bank statement? But offset and flexible mortgages can work well for the right people.

### Current-account mortgages

A CAM combines your current account, your mortgage, your savings and sometimes even your credit cards and personal loans into one all-purpose account. You pay your salary into this account, and any left over at the end of the month is used to reduce your mortgage. For example, if your net income is £2,000 a month and there is still £250 left over when the next month's salary arrives, that £250 comes off your mortgage. Of course, it only works for people who do have something left over each month.

Your overpayments are almost like savings because you can borrow them back. But by using them to reduce your mortgage debt and save yourself interest, you have earned more from them than you would in a conventional savings account. A CAM comes with a normal chequebook and debit card and you can withdraw money up to a set limit. The mortgage interest rate on CAMs is higher than average, but this is balanced by the fact that all your other borrowing is cheaper. Instead of shopping around for the cheapest loan to buy a new car, you would simply borrow the money from your CAM.

In theory, a CAM can save you lots of interest and help you pay off your mortgage early, because interest is calculated daily and every pound paid into the account reduces the amount of your loan. But a CAM will work for you only if you use it in the disciplined way it is meant to be used. Used unwisely (i.e. no salary left over each month and constant borrowings), it could lead to a bottomless pit of debt.

### Offset mortgages/intelligent finance

Offset mortgages are similar to CAMs, but your mortgage, current account, savings, personal loans and credit cards, though interconnected, are kept separate so you can see exactly where you are on each account. This type of mortgage is referred to as 'intelligent finance' by certain lenders.

The way it works is that you offset your savings and current account balances against your mortgage loan and other debts. For example, if you have a £50,000 home loan and £12,000 in your current account and savings, you will not pay interest on £12,000 of your home loan. And because you are not receiving interest on your current account and savings, there is no tax to pay. You can work the system the other way round. Instead of using your savings to reduce the amount of mortgage interest you pay, you can get the same rate of interest on your savings as you pay on your mortgage loan (up to the amount of the mortgage). As with a current-account mortgage, you pay for these privileges with higher interest rates.

Another version of this is the saver mortgage, which simply sets your savings against your mortgage loan so you pay interest on less of the loan. As with an offset mortgage, this can pay off your mortgage early because a higher proportion of your regular monthly payment (assuming this stays the same) goes towards reducing your debt. But bear in mind that offset and saver mortgages are really useful only to people who keep their current account in credit and have substantial savings.

## Flexible mortgages

Flexible mortgages have become very popular since they were first introduced in the mid-1990s. The reason they are so successful is that they put you in control of the way you manage the debt. You can underpay, overpay, take payment holidays and borrow back overpayments. Most mortgage lenders now have at least one flexible product on offer, though some are more flexible than others. The best ones allow:

- increases in your monthly payments. Even very small regular overpayments can knock a year or two off your mortgage term
- lump-sum repayments to reduce the loan. If you can afford to take advantage of this, it will enable you to save tens of thousands of pounds in interest and get rid of your mortgage early
- reduced monthly payments for a period of time. You are normally allowed to do this once you have made some overpayments. It is a useful facility for when you have extra expenses, but not for frequent use as it increases your debt again
- payment holidays, allowing you to make no payments for up to a year – a wonderful feature if you want to take a year off or go travelling. Some lenders only allow two-month breaks
- lump-sum withdrawals, allowing you to borrow back your overpayments. This allows you to treat your overpayments like an instant-access savings account. But by reducing your mortgage, they have earned you more than they would in a savings account

- no redemption penalties if you pay off your loan early, though you may still encounter them if the mortgage incorporates fixed or discounted rates
- daily calculation of interest, so every payment immediately reduces the amount of interest due. This saves a lot of money compared with the old system of calculating interest annually in arrears.

Some flexible mortgages take the concept a step further and combine all these features with offset or CAM facilities. The whole 'flexible' idea has caught on so fast that many conventional mortgages now include flexible features such as overpayments, underpayments and daily calculation of interest. However, it's important to be realistic about all this. If you know you are fairly unlikely to make lump-sum repayments or overpayments, it's probably not worth paying the higher interest rates that are charged on flexible mortgages.

But, handled well, they have many plus points, especially for the self-employed. When the money's there you can make overpayments that will pave the way for leaner times when you may want to reduce your payments or take a payment holiday.

## Remortgaging

Gone are the days when remortgaging (taking out a new mortgage on the same property) was seen as a desperate measure to which only people in real financial difficulty would resort. These days it makes excellent sense to shop around for a new mortgage if you can quite clearly see that other lenders are offering their borrowers better deals than yours. If interest rates are low and look like bottoming out, you might want to switch to a fixed-rate deal. Or you might want to unlock some of the capital tied up in your property to consolidate other debts or finance home improvements.

Your new mortgage doesn't even have to be with a new lender. If you've noticed that your existing lender is offering better rates to new borrowers, it's worth asking whether they would be prepared to offer you, too, a more competitive rate. If they can, it probably makes sense to stick with them because this will save you the cost of remortgaging. But if not, then it's time to switch lenders.

The first thing to do is ask your existing lender for a redemption statement. This should arrive by return of post and will tell you how much is outstanding on your loan and whether you will incur any penalties for paying it off. Redemption penalties usually apply only to fixed-rate and discount mortgages and may be payable for several months after the special-offer period has ended. If they just apply up to the end of the discounted period, you could arrange to switch on the day that you are due to change to the standard variable rate (SVR). If they go on longer, subtract the cost from the savings you will make by moving to a new lender to see if you would still be better off switching.

Apart from early redemption charges, the other usual costs of remortgaging include:

- valuation fee
- arrangement fee
- solicitor's fee and disbursements.

Although the average cost of remortgaging a £50,000 loan is around £750, some or all of these charges may be paid by your new lender as part of their remortgage package. Trawling around for the best deals can be very time-consuming but worth it in the long run. By just switching from a standard variable rate of 5.5 per cent to a five-year fixed rate of 4.5 per cent, you could save yourself several thousand pounds over the five-year fixed term. Look in the finance sections of national papers for 'best buy' mortgages, or consult a broker.

## Buy-to-let mortgages

These are specifically designed for people who are buying a property to let out to tenants. Interest rates are usually higher than for a home you are buying to live in, and the amount you can borrow is more dependent on the rent you will earn than on income. Lenders normally expect you to put down a 20 or 25 per cent deposit. There's more about buying to let in Chapter 7.

## Islamic mortgages

Most UK home loans involve the payment of interest, which is forbidden under Sharia law. However, there are now two UK lenders, the United Bank of Kuwait and the West Bromwich Building Society, who offer products that are compatible with Islamic law. These are based on Ijara and Murabaha methods.

### Ijara

Under this system, the customer chooses a home in the normal way and agrees a price with the vendor. The property is then purchased by the lender, who becomes its legal owner. The property is then sold on to the customer at the original price, with payments spread over an agreed period of time. During that time the customer pays the lender rent for the use of the property. Legal ownership of the property is transferred to the customer only at the end of the agreed period.

### Murabaha

Here again, the customer chooses a property and agrees a price in the normal way. The lender then buys the property, but immediately sells it on to the customer at a higher price. That price is determined by the value of the property, the amount of the first payment and the number of years it will take to repay the loan. Until now, the disadvantage of this system has been that stamp duty must be paid twice – once by the lender and then by the customer – but it was announced in the 2003 Budget that this will change. Once the double stamp duty is abolished, many more lenders will enter the Islamic mortgages market.

At the moment, these mortgages are expensive, although ways of making them cheaper are currently being investigated. They cannot be used to purchase properties under local authority 'right to buy' schemes.

# Insurance

**If you are buying a property as a couple or if anyone is dependent on you, it makes sense to have an insurance policy to pay off the loan if you (or your partner, if it's a joint mortgage) were to die.** Endowment and pension mortgages usually include life insurance, but repayment mortgages don't.

### Mortgage protection

Mortgage protection is a relatively cheap form of life insurance, because the amount the policy would have to pay out goes down as the amount you owe becomes less. Whatever kind of mortgage you have, take out a policy that covers your mortgage payments in the event of accident, illness or redundancy.

### Buildings insurance

Lenders also require you to have buildings insurance as a condition of the mortgage. This is to protect against things such as damage by fire, storm, flood and subsidence. It covers the structure of the house and permanent fixtures and fittings like baths, basins, kitchen units, fences, walls and patios. Many lenders arrange this for you and include the premium in your monthly payment. But you should also be free to shop around for buildings insurance.

# Problems with mortgage payments

**There was a time not so long ago when mortgage lenders would repossess homes at the drop of a hat.** Fortunately this situation improved with the introduction of the mortgage code in 1997, and lenders now have to 'consider cases of financial difficulty and mortgage arrears sympathetically and positively'. But repossession is still a risk if you fall too far behind with your mortgage payments.

It is important to have mortgage-protection insurance from the start (this costs around £5 for every £100 of monthly payment) because home-buyers get less state help than renters if they lose their job. Even if your mortgage depends on two salaries you will not get housing benefit if your partner is still working, and home-buyers who claim income support get no state help with their mortgage for the first nine months of their claim.

To avoid losing your home, bear the following points in mind:

- If you fall behind with your payments, contact your mortgage lender at once before they contact you
- Contact your local Citizens' Advice Bureau for advice on dealing with debt
- Reply promptly to any letters from your mortgage lender so they don't think you are burying your head in the sand
- Ask your local social-security office to help with interest payments (they will not help with capital repayments)
- Consider renting out your property if the rent would cover your mortgage bills and some living costs. You will need your lender's permission to do this, and there will be tax to pay on any net profit after you have subtracted your mortgage payments and other costs
- It would be better for you to sell your home yourself than have it repossessed. You would get more money from the sale and would not have a black mark on your credit record. Your mortgage lender will have to agree to the sale
- If you are taken to court, attend the hearing to explain your circumstances – don't just write a letter. If you sound as if you are likely to be able to get a job and clear the arrears, the court will suspend the possession order.

## Complaints against a lender

If your lender has caused you financial loss or delayed your transaction through mistakes or misinformation, send a letter of complaint to the head office. If the response is unsatisfactory, you can take your complaint to the Building Societies Ombudsman or the Financial Ombudsman Service (see page 172).

# 4

# Finding your property

**Once you know the maximum amount you can pay for a property (taking into account your deposit, your mortgage and all the horrible hidden costs of moving such as stamp duty), sit down and make a realistic checklist of your 'must-haves' and 'would-likes'.**

The must-haves will be absolute prerequisites – things you are not prepared to compromise on. The would-likes will be features you hope to find but accept you might have to do without (for example, snooker rooms and saunas!). These lists will depend on your likes and dislikes, and also on your lifestyle. If you have children, then schools and parks are a priority; if you have a cat you may need a garden; if you are a sun-worshipper, the garden needs to be south- or west-facing; dogs require a place to be taken for walks; a car has to be parked; a bicycle has to be kept somewhere. List your requirements in order of priority.

For a house, your considerations might be:

**Must-haves**

- Victorian/newly built/1930s semi
- easy journey to work
- three bedrooms
- kitchen you can eat in
- central heating
- space for piano
- garage
- good-sized living room
- good state of decoration
- kitchen doesn't need work
- some sort of garden
- quiet area
- near schools and parks
- near transport and shops
- feeling of space.

**Would-likes**

- study or playroom
- fireplace and period features
- lots of storage space
- good-sized rooms
- semi-detached
- opportunities for improvement (possible extension, loft room, second bathroom)
- back entrance for bike
- plenty of light
- south- or west-facing garden
- open outlook
- near sports club or gym.

For a flat, your considerations might be:

**Must-haves**

- 90+ year lease
- ground floor/first floor/top floor
- purpose-built/conversion
- good security
- well-maintained communal parts
- open plan, with separate kitchen
- entryphone
- lift.

**Would-likes**

- balcony/patio
- share of freehold
- good soundproofing
- nice view
- use of garden
- parking space.

For a country property your lists might also include:

**Must-haves**

- near/in a village
- period property
- rural views
- away from main road
- mains drainage
- large/manageable garden
- outbuildings
- sheltered position
- not likely to flood.

**Would-likes**

- thatched roof
- roses round door
- inglenook fireplace
- Aga
- no visible/audible neighbours
- paddock for pony
- unconverted barn or wreck to do up.

Try not to let the must-have list become too long, or you may never find a property that's acceptable to you. Few people find a home that meets all their requirements at the right price, so be prepared to compromise – even about one or two of your must-haves. And remember to use your imagination! Many properties that appear to lack certain essential features could easily be made to have them. Utility rooms can be knocked into kitchens to create eating areas, kitchens can be revamped without buying new units, dark rooms look a lot lighter with a coat of pale emulsion. Obviously it's tempting to buy a place that is just how you want it, but bear in mind that a house or flat that you can improve is always a better investment.

When you know exactly what you're hoping to find, explore your chosen neighbourhood to pinpoint the specific areas where you are most likely to find it. Look in local free papers and estate agents' windows to give yourself an idea of what's available for your kind of money. If you're house-hunting in a city, buy an *A–Z* and make a note of the roads that do and don't appeal. This will save a lot of time when an agent rings to say they've got just the little flat you are looking for in Willow Avenue. You will immediately know that this is the busy street that backs on to the railway line with the sewage works opposite.

Spend lots and lots of time driving, cycling or walking around. Investigate highways and byways, lanes, alleys and cul-de-sacs. Look around the back of possible locations to see what is lurking there, find things out from local people in shops and pubs. If you already know someone who lives in your chosen patch, enlist their help because they're more likely to know the pros and cons of the place, and can also tell you if a new property suddenly comes on the market. You could also research things like council-tax charges and crime rates, as these vary from district to district.

When you've researched the area and the property market, and have decided what you want and can afford, you're ready to start looking at properties. This is the fun bit.

# Ways of finding properties

**From estate agents' lists to dropping leaflets through letterboxes – there are many different ways to track down that elusive property, and it's worth trying them all.**

### Estate agents

You will find the names and addresses of local estate agents in the property pages of local papers and the Yellow Pages. It's worth approaching every agent in the district, since a lot of sellers put their property with a sole agent. Most agents display a selection of properties in their window, with photographs, but not everything on their books will be there, so do go inside to register and find out what's newly on the market or about to come up.

Give each agent a very clear idea of your requirements – the type of property, number of bedrooms and so on. Let them know what you definitely don't want, but try not to be too narrow or specific or you might not get sent details of properties that would actually have interested you. If you don't have time to drop in, you can phone, fax or e-mail your enquiry. Most estate agents now have websites that list the properties they have in each price range, though these tend not to give much detail or even the exact location.

An agent will want to know your price range and whether:
- you are a first-time buyer
- your own property is sold or under offer
- you are a cash buyer or will need a mortgage.

Some people treat looking at properties as an amusing hobby, so the more ready-to-go and serious you seem, the more estate agents will put themselves out to help you. Whenever a desirable house or flat comes on the market, an agent will always offer it first to a buyer who is in a position to proceed without any delays. But whatever your situation is, it makes sense to establish a good relationship with several agents. Follow up your first contact with regular phone calls and visits so you are at the front of their mind when that perfect property comes up.

However specific you are about the kind of property you want, you will be sent details of lots you are not remotely interested in. There's no way round this because agents say people often end up buying a home that is nothing like what they originally asked for (and, after all, unwanted property particulars are easy to bin).

Estate agents don't charge fees to buyers as they are paid an agreed commission by the vendor on completion of the sale. The only exception is a finder's or relocation agent. If you are house-hunting from a distance, this type of agent can find a property for you and negotiate the purchase. The charge for this service is usually a flat fee of around £300 plus 1 per cent of the purchase price at the end of a successful transaction.

### Estate agents' details

The particulars that estate agents compile to describe properties have long been the butt of jokes. This is partly because they use language that no one else uses – like 'wash-hand basin' and 'vanitory unit' – and also because you have to read between the lines. 'Compact' means tiny, 'in need of a little cosmetic improvement' means the paper is hanging off the walls and 'close to all amenities' probably means slap, bang on the high street.

The purpose of these details is to persuade you to go and look at the property so, if you want to avoid wasted journeys, become aware of hidden meanings and look out for omissions. If a property is in a quiet tree-lined road the details will say so – though you must still make sure for yourself that the road isn't the local rat-run. Legislation has stopped agents saying things that are actually untrue but, as we all know, there are many different ways of telling the truth, so do check everything, especially the measurements, for yourself.

Before arranging to view a property, ask the agent about anything important to you that has not been specified. What does it look out on? Does the 'small patio' have some usable space, or is it just somewhere to keep dustbins?

Estate agents have done a lot to clean up their act since 1998, when a new code of practice was introduced. However, gazumping (when a vendor goes back on an agreement to sell and accepts a higher offer) is still 'legal'. And be wary of agents who tell you that your offer can't be passed on because the seller is already considering another, higher, offer. The higher offer may not exist and, in any case, a seller should be told about every offer.

## The Internet

Over the past two years, according to the Halifax, there has been a tenfold increase in the number of people using the Internet to look for homes. Some websites, like rightmove.co.uk, fish4.co.uk and assertahome.com, are huge databases of properties being sold by hundreds of different estate agents. Others bring buyers and sellers together directly, cutting out agents altogether. These normally charge sellers a fixed fee to put details and photographs of their property on the site, together with a contact phone number and e-mail address. Among the biggest are Houseweb, Property Broker, The Little House

Company, Homeowner Sales and easier.co.uk. (See the list on page 173.)

You type your requirements – location, price, number of bedrooms – into the site's search facility, and are shown brief details of any matching (or vaguely matching) properties. You then click on the ones that interest you to see more details and perhaps a selection of interior and exterior pictures. To find out more or arrange a viewing, you contact the owner.

It's also worth searching the property pages of *Loot's* website, www.loot.com, or thisislondon.co.uk, the London *Evening Standard* website. Most property websites also have links to online conveyancing and mortgage services, which are fine for experienced buyers who anticipate a simple transaction, but not so good if you are new to the property market or if your situation is complicated – in which case it's better to deal with people face to face.

## Local and national papers

Lots of owners advertise privately in the 'Property for Sale' columns of local and national newspapers and magazines, and free-ad papers like *Loot*, especially during housing booms. When it's a seller's market, it's important to buy the paper as early as possible on the day of publication and arrange to view any homes that interest you at once. When the market is slow, an owner may be advertising privately because he or she is getting no results from an agent.

These publications also have 'Property Wanted' columns, so you could put in an ad specifying exactly what you are looking for. Local papers are much cheaper to advertise in than nationals, and remember to include any information that will appeal to sellers such as 'no chain' or 'cash buyer'. Private advertisers are not paying commission to an estate agent so they may accept a lower offer.

## 'For Sale' boards

Boards are put up by both estate agents and private sellers. New ones go up every day, so keep looking out for them in your chosen area. But don't go knocking on the doors of flats or houses that are for sale as this will annoy the owners (though you may get away with a friendly enquiry if the owner is out weeding the front garden on a sunny Sunday afternoon). Normally, you should ring the number on the board to ask for details or make an appointment to view.

## Leafleting

One of the more enterprising ways to find a property is to drop leaflets through doors in the road or roads that most interest you. Make it abundantly clear that you are a private buyer and no commission will be payable. If someone is already thinking about selling and you succeed in striking a deal, you will have saved them trouble and money.

# Viewing and choosing

**There's an art to viewing properties, as you have only a short time in which to take in lots of different things.** For a start, don't try to see too many places at once or you will get them muddled up.

You"ll find you waste less time looking at unsuitable properties if you:
- read the details very carefully
- ring up and ask the agent (or owner if it's a private sale) about any important points that need clarifying. (Which side of the road is it on? Is it overshadowed by that office block? Does a lot of work need doing?)
- drive past the outside before arranging to view. This will rule out a lot of properties that look OK on paper, but whose exteriors or location wouldn't actually suit you at all.

When you go to view a property, take with you:
- the estate agent's particulars – you may need to consult them
- a notebook and pen to jot down any comments or queries
- a measuring tape so you can check any important dimensions for yourself, as agents tend to measure into shelves and alcoves.

You don't need to take in every tiny detail the first time you visit a property, because if you are really interested you will go back. First impressions tell you a lot and you will probably know straight away if the property is not for you. In that case make your visit as short as possible (without seeming rude), as there's no point in wasting your or the vendor's time asking pointless question about fixtures and fittings and council tax if the house doesn't interest you. Try not to be influenced by furniture and decor that you would never have chosen, because that won't be there when you are. Instead, try to imagine yourself living in the property.

If your first impression is favourable (many people fall instantly in love with their future homes), try not to get so swept away that you make an offer there and then. Consider the property very carefully in the light of your checklist. Obviously not everything will be perfect, but questions to ask yourself include:
- Could you realistically live there?
- Is the accommodation what you need?
- Can you afford any work that clearly needs doing immediately?

- How close is the property to the facilities you need?
- Is there room for your favourite bits of furniture?
- Is there enough storage space/potential storage space?
- Are the heating, lighting and electrical fittings in good order?
- What are the plumbing and bathroom fittings like?
- How much redecoration will you have to do?
- Is there enough natural light in the rooms?
- Could you cook/eat in the kitchen? Are there enough work surfaces and cupboards?
- Is there plumbing for a washing machine/dishwasher?
- Are there signs/smells of damp or mould, especially in a basement?
- What is the general condition of the building?
- Is the garden big or small enough for your lifestyle?

If you are really interested, find out as much as you can from the seller:
- How long have they lived in the property?
- How long has it been on the market? (They're more likely to accept an offer if it's been for sale for a while.)
- What work have they had done?
- When was the boiler/central-heating system installed?
- What improvements would they make if they were staying?
- When does the garden get the sun?
- What are the neighbours like?
- What are the outgoings – council tax, ground rent, service charges?
- Is it easy to park? Do you need a permit?
- Have they found a new home to move to – if so, when will the house/flat be available?
- What fixtures and fittings are included in the price?
- Have they ever been burgled?
- What are the local schools like?

Some people also ask the seller why they are moving, although this is quite a nosy question and not really a buyer's business. Fine if it's because they need a bigger place or their work has moved 200 miles away – not so fine if the sale is to do with death, divorce or disaster. In any case, if the reason is something that would concern you, like they can't afford to renew the roof or their car keeps getting vandalized, they are highly unlikely to tell you. But you could ask where they are moving to and their answer might reveal the reason for the sale.

Nosiness is fine, however, when it comes to the property itself.

- Look inside cupboards, under furniture, even behind wall hangings if you think they may be concealing something.
- Be suspicious of polystyrene tiles on ceilings, woodchip wallpaper and brand-new patches of paint that are different from the surrounding area – they may be hiding cracks or damp patches. Damp patches on ceilings indicate a leaking roof.
- Take a good look at the exterior – roof, brickwork, doors, window frames, guttering, downpipes – and notice any cracks in interior or exterior walls.

But don't overdo the DIY structural survey, even if you know what you are doing. Owners don't appreciate having corners of carpets ripped up or amateurs' screwdrivers poked into their walls and window frames. The main purpose of this inspection is to give yourself a fair idea of the property's condition so you can judge what kind of offer to make and be aware of any specific problems you should mention to your surveyor.

It's always important to be diplomatic as vendors prefer to sell to people they like. If you're being shown round by an estate agent you can say whatever you choose but, if the vendor is within earshot, remember it's their home and try to avoid exclaiming (or whispering) about the ghastliness of the colours.

Gut feelings count for everything in house-hunting and you will probably know straight away if this is the home for you. But be careful not to give too much away. There's no harm in telling the owner that you like it a lot, but don't say you definitely want to buy it, because if they know you are desperately keen they may not consider an offer below the asking price.

However certain you are, it's essential to view the property at least once more, preferably with a friend or relative who won't be living there as they will be more objective. Ideally, on this second visit, you want to be able to wander round on your own, without the owner or estate agent breathing down your neck. If this isn't possible, don't let yourself be rushed. Look at everything you want to look at, and jot down any important comments or queries.

If you still love the property after your second visit, return to the location (you needn't go inside) at various different times of day – morning, evening, rush hour, after closing time – to make sure the ambience is still the same. Take a walk around the immediate vicinity to satisfy yourself that there's no serious blight, like a noisy factory. When you get home, refer to your checklist to see how closely the property matches your needs and what important compromises you would be making.

Once you are totally convinced that this is where you want to live, waste no time in making an offer.

## What to look out for when buying your first flat

- Are there names on all the doorbells? Blank spaces indicate rented flats.
- The state of the floors, walls, ceilings and stairways in the communal parts of the building will tell you a lot about the management agreement.
- Check communal areas, inside and out, for litter or heaps of junk mail.
- Check that the intercom (and the lift if there is one) work – there could be a lot of stairs between the front door and your flat.
- Listen for, and ask about, noise from neighbouring flats, especially in a converted house.
- Beware of flimsy walls between you and your neighbours. You can hear everything through them and, when fastening things to walls, you may go straight through to next door.
- Is there a parking space/access to the garden?
- Find out how long the last two owners lived in the flat – a high turnover may be a warning sign of problems to come.
- Make sure you know how long the lease is. Estate agents' details don't always include this information, although they should.
- Find out what the service and maintenance charges are, and if there's anything they don't cover (such as repainting the exterior).

## Tips on viewing an older house

Older houses always have a few problems. Unless these are serious, they needn't stop you buying the property, but knowing about them will put you in a better bargaining position. Don't rely on just a valuation report on an older property – always get a home-buyer report or, for really old or neglected houses, a full structural survey.

Before making an offer:

- Look carefully (with binoculars) at the condition of the roof and chimney stack – are any slates or tiles missing? If possible, go into the roof space with a torch – can you see daylight? Is there any evidence of leaks?
- Inspect flat roofs for torn, cracked or blistered felt, torn or damaged flashing and standing puddles
- Check the main walls for bulges and cracks. Old cracks may not be a problem, but new ones could mean the house needs underpinning – very expensive
- What is the external decoration (especially the woodwork) like?
- Check the state of the gutters and drainpipes – leaks can cause penetrating damp
- Notice the condition of doors and windows – look for rot in door or window frames, cracked paint and missing putty in frames and sills

- Are the floors level? Floors that slope or move a lot indicate bad construction or subsidence
- Look for cracks or holes in walls and ceilings, loose or damaged floorboards, wobbly handrails
- Inspect the internal woodwork of the property for signs of rot or telltale tiny woodworm holes
- Look for any damp patches on walls, floors or ceilings. You can hire a damp meter if you suspect a problem
- Ask if any major work (new roof, underpinning, repointing, new windows, new damp-proof course, rewiring, replumbing) has been done recently. Are there any guarantees?

## Tricks used in show houses

Show houses – or 'viewhomes' as some are now called – are big business. Not only do they sell homes, they're also hot properties themselves, with people queuing to buy them complete with fixtures and fittings, right down to the cups and saucers in the kitchens. But these dream homes are not always quite what they seem, as all sorts of tricks can be used to make them seem more desirable. For example:

- TVs and hi-fis left out of living rooms because there's no room for them
- undersized furniture used to create an impression of more space
- interior doors left off to make rooms seem bigger
- no wardrobe in a small bedroom because there's nowhere to put one
- horizontal striped wallpaper used to make rooms look bigger
- curtains made too narrow for windows and left open for maximum light
- concealed lighting left permanently on in rooms that are too dark
- kitchens with space for only one appliance (i.e. a washing machine or a dishwasher but not both).

# Making an offer

**This is a tricky business as a lot depends on the state of the property market and how badly you want the flat or house.** If things are selling fast and the property is realistically priced, you may have to offer the asking price or very near it. But if it has been on the market for weeks or months, you could try a lower offer – though not insultingly low or the vendor won't want to be bothered with you.

You can make your offer direct to the seller as long as there is no suggestion that you are trying to bypass the agent (who would still be entitled to claim his commission). But, unless it's a private sale, it is probably best to go through the agent who is, in theory, experienced at handling negotiations.

Before making your offer, decide on the absolute top price you are prepared to pay. Then offer about 10 per cent less so there is room for manoeuvre. The estate agent is obliged to pass your offer on to the seller even if he or she knows it will be rejected. The offer doesn't commit you to anything, provided it is made 'subject to contract and survey'. If a survey reveals a fault that will be costly to put right, you can reduce your offer to take account of this.

If you have offered quite a lot less than the asking price tell the estate agent why, so he or she can pass this information on to the seller. Perhaps you think the property is overpriced or needs a lot of work. Use the flaws you noted when you were looking round the house as ammunition. An offer can be made by phone or in person, but it's a good idea to confirm it writing so everyone has a record of it. There may be quite a bit of toing and froing after this before you do or don't come to an agreement. If someone else is after the same property, try not to get into a 'bidding war' because you could end up paying more than the house is worth. Make your final offer and then, if necessary, walk away.

If you're close to a deal on a property you really want, don't continue haggling down to the last penny because this creates bad feeling. In any negotiation, both sides need to feel they have done well and, if possible, you want to remain on good terms with your vendor right up to completion. You don't want them removing all the light bulbs (or worse) just to spite you!

Once your offer has been accepted 'subject to contract and survey', you may be asked for a small, returnable deposit to show good faith (especially if you want the property to be taken off the market and not shown to anyone else) but you are not obliged to pay this. If you do and the sale falls through before contracts are exchanged, the preliminary deposit has to be repaid.

Agreed sales should be confirmed in writing by the estate agent, or by the vendor if it's a private sale. Now is the time to:

- tell your mortgage lender the purchase price, so they can arrange a valuation and agree your loan
- give your solicitor or conveyancer the address of the property, details of the vendor's solicitor (available from the estate agent) and the name and address of your mortgage lender
- arrange for a home-buyer's report/survey on the property, if this is not being done through your lender.

Remember that (in England and Wales) there is nothing to stop either you or the vendor pulling out, right up to the moment you exchange contracts.

## Sealed bids

Instead of offering a property at a fixed asking price, agents sometimes get each would-be buyer to write down the maximum price they are prepared to pay, seal it in an envelope and hand it in by a given date. The highest bidder normally gets the house – although other things, such as how ready you are to proceed, may be taken into consideration.

This system is sometimes used when houses and flats are selling like hot cakes, or if an agent thinks there is going to be a lot of competition for a property. It's especially common when a large neglected house that's ripe for conversion comes on the market and property developers are hovering like flies. Unfortunately, private buyers seldom get a look-in in these circumstances.

The difficulty with sealed bids is that you have no idea what other people are offering, although the agent should be willing to give you an indication of what he or she thinks the property is worth. If you're very keen, try bidding an odd amount that is slightly over the odds, like £211,333. Most people offer a nice round sum like £210,000, so you might win by £1,333 (or not). Remember to mention anything that might tip the scales in your favour – like you are a cash buyer or don't have to sell another property.

### First-time buyer tip
New carpets, curtains and appliances are expensive, so see if the vendor is prepared to throw them in at a small extra cost – this does not have to be part of the purchase price. There may even be some useful furniture going. These items may not be exactly what you would choose, but will save you money in those expensive first years of home-ownership.

# Timing

**If you are selling as well as buying, timing is crucial. Should you find a new place first, then put your old home on the market?** Or should you get your current home under offer before you start looking for a new one? (Answer: get your old home under offer first.)

There's no harm in looking in estate agents' windows to see what's around before you sell. However, it's a waste of emotion to set your heart on a place and then find you can't sell your current home quickly enough to buy it. Also, you may not know how much you can spend on a new property until you know exactly what you're getting for the old one.

If you do fall in love with a new place before you have sold you can certainly put in an offer, but no one will take you very seriously until you have found a buyer for your own property. At this stage you are still a bird in the bush, and vendors – unless they are personal friends or in no hurry – prefer a bird in the hand and will almost certainly go on showing the property to other people. Assuming both homes are in the same area, it makes sense to ask the selling agent to handle your sale as well. The prospect of two commissions will make him/her pull out all the stops to bring off both sales. But make sure your property isn't undervalued or undersold in the process.

Problems with 'chains' – when one side of a deal can't proceed because their buyer's buyer (or even their buyer's buyer's buyer) has been delayed – are one of the most frustrating aspects of buying and selling property. They very often lead to sales falling through so, however sure you are that your buyer is reliable, don't ever be persuaded to exchange contracts on your purchase before doing so on your sale. If you do, and then find yourself unable to proceed, you can be sued for the full purchase price. Some buyers in this awful situation take out a bridging loan to pay for the new property, hoping that it will be only a matter of weeks before their house or flat is sold. But it could take months (or even years!) and meanwhile you will be paying heavy interest on the loan as well as your mortgage payments. So don't even think about a bridging loan if contracts on your sale haven't been exchanged – it could ruin you.

Even exchanging contracts on your sale first can create difficulties if, for any reason, your purchase falls through. Some people decide to exchange on their sale before they have found a property to buy, and move into rented accommodation while looking. The risk here is that property prices could go up between your sale and your purchase. And funds that could have gone towards your new home will be going down the drain in rent.

The ideal is to exchange contracts on both properties at the same time on the same day. If, after both sets of contracts have been exchanged, you need to complete your purchase before your sale (so you can get essential building work done before you move in, for example), you could consider getting a short-term bridging loan to tide you over. But remember, this is expensive.

## TIMING – CASE STUDY

**Joan K thought she had timed her sale and purchase to perfection and that both would be completed on the same day. Everything went smoothly until she was informed, just a few days before exchange, that her vendors had received a higher offer and were going to take it unless she could equal it. The higher price was much more than she could afford, so she decided to let herself be gazumped and to move herself, her two children and three cats into an unfurnished, rented garden flat until she could find another place to buy.**

The only suitable flat she could find required her to sign a shorthold tenancy agreement for a full year, but this didn't seem such a bad idea as it would give her plenty of time to find another property. What Joan hadn't reckoned on was a sudden and alarming rise in property prices, which meant that if she didn't buy a new home very quickly she might be priced out of the market. It didn't take long to find a place she liked and her quite low offer was accepted on the understanding that she could move swiftly because she was not in a chain. The only problem was her lease, which still had nine months to run. There was a chance that the landlord would let her leave at the six-month mark if she gave him two months' notice, but he refused, so Joan ended up paying six months' rent for a flat she wasn't living in. The situation was annoying but, as prices in her area were rising at around 2.5 per cent a month, she was right not to delay her purchase any longer.

# Home Information Packs – a new way of buying and selling

**The home-buying and -selling process in England and Wales is currently one of the slowest in Europe, with failures and delays costing consumers up to £350 million a year.** A staggering 28 per cent of transactions fall through because of the time it takes to arrange surveys and local authority searches and obtain answers to queries – or because the results of these surveys, searches and queries are unsatisfactory.

The main problem with the present system is that much of the key information you need to help you make the decision to buy becomes available only after you have agreed to buy. At the time of your offer, you don't actually know what condition the property is in, whether it's going to be affected by local road or building developments, what conditions are attached to it (such as rights of way), or even whether the so-called vendor is entitled to sell it.

All this will change when the new Home Information Packs become law, estimated by the Office of the Deputy Prime Minister to be in 2006. These packs form part of the government's new Housing Bill and – assuming they fulfil their promise – will make the whole home-buying and -selling process faster, more transparent and more consumer friendly, leading to less stress and fewer wasted costs. Once introduced, they will be compulsory, as a single missing pack in a chain would cancel out the benefits of all the others.

## How it will work

Before putting a home on the market, the vendor will be required to put together a pack of information for prospective buyers. This will contain much of the data that is currently provided later in the transaction, for example:

- terms of sale (freehold or leasehold)
- evidence of title (proof of ownership)
- replies to standard preliminary enquiries made on behalf of buyers (such as a list of fixtures and fittings)
- copies of any planning, listed building and building regulations consents and approvals
- (for new properties) copies of warranties and guarantees
- any guarantees for work carried out on the property
- replies to local authority searches
- a home condition report based on a professional survey, including an energy efficiency assessment.

Plus, for leasehold properties:

- a copy of the lease
- most recent service-charge accounts and receipts
- building-insurance policy details and payment receipts
- regulations made by the landlord of the management company.

The packs are rather like an MOT on a car, in that they identify any problems before you sell (giving you the chance to put them right) and remain valid for a fixed period of time. Sales should go through more swiftly and certainly because there will be less risk of renegotiation after an offer has been accepted.

Since few sellers would want to be bothered with assembling the pack themselves, this service will be provided by estate agents, lenders or law firms at a cost of around £700. But once a pack has been commissioned and assembled, it will be the property of the owner, so he or she can switch agents or sell the property privately if they want to.

As part of the same package of reforms:

- Buyers are being encouraged to obtain 'in principle' mortgage offers before making an offer on a property
- Lenders are being called upon to provide a faster and more efficient service
- Property professionals are being encouraged to use the latest information technology so that information can be exchanged quickly and economically.

Possible disadvantages of Home Information Packs may be:

- The packs will add considerably to sellers' moving costs. But they will reduce legal and survey costs on the property being bought so the end result should be much the same
- It remains to be seen whether all mortgage lenders and purchasers will be satisfied with a survey commissioned by the seller. The Council of Mortgage Lenders is currently devising a certification scheme which should ensure that no further valuation is needed
- Surveys on older properties may not be as thorough as you would like, so you may still have to pay, and wait, for another one
- The cost of the packs may make people in areas with low property prices more reluctant to sell
- There is no information yet about when prospective purchasers would see the pack. In order to be fully informed, they would need to see it (perhaps in the estate agent's office) before their first viewing
- When sellers decide to put right any defects mentioned in the pack, they will have to pay for an inspector to return and supply a further certificate.

### First-time buyer tip

Home Information Packs will making home-buying cheaper for you. You will save several hundred pounds in legal and survey costs and, because you aren't selling, you won't have to pay for a pack yourself.

# Buying at auction

**Auctions are the places to find interesting and unusual properties, but this method of buying a home is strictly for those who know their own mind as, once the hammer falls on your bid, you can't back out.** Even if you were to turn tail and run without signing anything, you would still have to buy the property.

Details of properties for sale by auction are advertised by estate agents in the normal way, but the particulars usually take the form of a brochure and contain much more information. Make sure your finance is in place, as once your bid is accepted you have to put down 10 per cent of the price immediately, and pay the balance within 28 days.

You must also get your survey, searches and preliminary enquiries done before the date of the auction, as it's too late to say there is something wrong with the property afterwards. These expenses are lost, obviously, if you don't end up buying the property. As an incentive, many sellers provide the information up front (rather like Home Information Packs) and then pass the costs on to the successful bidder.

It's easy to get carried away at an auction, so it's essential to decide in advance what you think the property is worth and the maximum amount you are prepared to pay. Write the figure down and don't let yourself go above it in the heat of the moment.

There is often a 'reserve' price on a property – this is the minimum price that the seller will consider. The property will be withdrawn if it doesn't reach its reserve price, but you may be able to do a deal with the seller afterwards. Some sellers are open to offers before the auction.

# Buying in Scotland

**Scotland has its own legal system, and Scottish property transactions are quite different from those in England and Wales.**

Property sales in Scotland begin with an exchange of solicitors' letters, called the negotiation of missives, and the contract becomes legally binding when this short exchange ends (the conclusion of missives). After this there is no backing out, unless one of the conditions in the missives is not met (for example, if the vendor doesn't own the property), when costs and damages would be payable. When buying from England, it's important to use a Scottish solicitor (and vice versa). Word-of-mouth recommendation is best but, failing this, the Law Society of Scotland has a Directory of General Services that lists solicitors.

Because things happen very quickly once a price has been agreed, purchasers need to have their survey completed and their mortgage in place before their solicitor makes a formal written offer. The period between the formal offer and the conclusion of missives is similar to the period before exchange of contracts in England, but gazumping and gazundering are more or less impossible because a written offer is a legal document and missives are usually concluded within one or two weeks.

There are no long leases in Scotland. All property, including flats, is owned outright, though certain conditions regarding use and alterations may have been put in place by the original landowner. When viewing a flat, look carefully at the condition of the building and make sure that the cost of repairs to the structure and communal parts is shared equally between all the flat-owners. This will be set out in the title deeds.

## Order of events

1. You arrange to view a property that has been advertised for sale – often by a solicitor doubling as an estate agent. Fixed prices do exist, but normally the price quoted (called the upset price) is the lowest that will be accepted and offers over it are invited.
2. Tell your solicitor that you are thinking of buying the property (you may or may not have an informal agreement about price at this stage, but on no account put anything in writing). He/she will contact the seller's solicitor to note an interest in the property. This means you will be kept informed of any developments, as there may be competing offers.
3. You arrange a survey and organize your mortgage.

4.  Your solicitor sends a formal offer (missive of sale) to the seller's solicitor, including enquiries about title, contents included in the sale, local searches and the move-in date – normally six to eight weeks after the offer.

5.  Assuming no one else has offered more, the seller's solicitor either accepts your offer and conditions or starts negotiating (a qualified acceptance). Several letters may now go back and forth (negotiation of missives) until full agreement is reached.

6.  When everyone is in agreement, your solicitor sends a letter of acceptance to the seller's solicitor. This is the conclusion of missives and the contract is now binding.

7.  Your solicitor draws up a new title deed, called a disposition, and conducts the necessary searches.

8.  The disposition is signed by the seller.

9.  If all the conditions of the sale are satisfied, the purchase price is paid and the disposition and the keys are handed over. After completion, a stamp duty of 1 per cent is payable.

10. Your title deed is registered in the Land Register, or sometimes the older (and less reliable) Register of Sazines.

There are disadvantages to the Scottish system. While it is quicker than the English or Welsh one, its main drawback is that it is almost impossible to co-ordinate your sale and purchase. People who complete their sale before their purchase often have to move into temporary accommodation, while those who buy before they sell frequently have to arrange bridging finance.

## HOUSE-HUNTING – CASE STUDY

**Sally M started house-hunting the day she put her own property on the market and found the place she wanted to buy far too early. She was happy to offer the asking price because the house was just what she was looking for, but realized there was no chance her offer would be accepted as she was nowhere near finding a buyer for her own property. A few days later her dream home went under offer to someone else.**

Six months later Sally finally found a buyer, but he wanted to complete within six weeks. She had temporarily stopped house-hunting and had nowhere to move to but, just on the off chance, decided to enquire again about the house she had liked so much before. To her delight, the agent informed her that the previous sale had just fallen through. Sally's offer was accepted within hours, she exchanged within four weeks and moved in a fortnight after that.

# 5

# After the offer

There's nothing more exciting than the moment when you realize that the home for which you have been so anxiously negotiating is finally 'under offer' – to YOU. All you need now is:

- a good solicitor or conveyancer
- a satisfactory survey
- a firm mortgage offer

… and nothing to go wrong with your sale.

# Conveyancing

**'Conveyancing' is the term commonly used for the entire legal and administrative process of transferring the ownership of property.** Unfortunately it's a process during which all sorts of things can go pear-shaped. Although it is rare for such nasties as undisclosed bankruptcies, unexpected sitting tenants, or vendors who don't have the right to sell to be discovered, all sorts of other problems can crop up – disputes over boundaries and fences, extensions that never had planning permission, squabbles over access or rights of way.

Before going ahead with a purchase, you need to know that:
- the vendor really owns the property
- there are no plans for developments that will affect the property
- there are no outstanding disputes regarding the property
- there are no unduly restrictive conditions attached to the property
- there are no undisclosed charges or mortgages against the property.

It is the job of the conveyancer to unearth any such complications and, if possible, resolve them. The conveyancing wheels tend to grind slowly, even at the best of times, so you need someone who will not drag their feet (or cut corners).

Your options are:
- do-it-yourself
- a licensed conveyancer
- a solicitor.

## DIY conveyancing

Lawyers tend to raise despairing eyebrows when they discover they will be dealing with a DIY conveyancer, but there is absolutely no legal reason why you shouldn't do your own conveyancing if you are confident and knowledgeable enough. There are a number of guides that will take you step by step through the process – make sure you use one that is bang up to date. Remember that if you do opt for DIY, your mortgage lender will still want to employ a solicitor to protect their interests in the property, and you will have to pay for this.

Although doing it yourself might save you money, it's quite time-consuming – and if you get something wrong, you won't be able to demand compensation from anyone else. Conveyancing may be routine work for a solicitor, but it is fairly difficult and technical for an amateur. Also, it is not the actual solicitor's bill that pushes up property-buying costs, so much as land-registry fees, stamp duty and search fees – which you will have to pay anyway.

Don't do your own conveyancing if:

- you are buying a leasehold flat or house
- you are buying in Scotland
- you're a first-time buyer with no experience of the property market (unless you are a law student!)
- the land is unregistered.

## Licensed conveyancers

Licensed conveyancers (who do not exist in Scotland) are specialist property lawyers who are trained and qualified in all aspects of the law dealing with property. They are not as qualified as solicitors in other aspects of law, but provide a full property-buying service and operate the same safeguards to protect the public. The profession was created by an Act of Parliament in 1985, but there are still not nearly as many conveyancers as solicitors. Conveyancers are usually cheaper, but the difference in price is not great, as solicitors' charges came down considerably when competition was introduced. If you choose a conveyancer, your lender may still insist on a qualified solicitor to handle their side of things.

## Solicitors

Solicitors deal with all kinds of legal issues, including conveyancing. The problem with solicitors who take on a full range of legal work is that they are often in court and out of touch just when you need them to react quickly to a situation. Beware, too, of having your entire transaction handed over to a trainee solicitor fresh out of law school – not what you need at all!

## Choosing your solicitor or conveyancer

Changing an incompetent solicitor or conveyancer halfway through a property transaction is likely to slow things down even further, so it's essential to choose wisely in the first place. You need someone who is quick and efficient, has plenty of experience of residential conveyancing and really knows the ropes.

The best way to find someone who is reasonable and reliable, and who will give you the guidance and support you need, is through the personal recommendation of a friend. Failing this, your estate agent or mortgage lender will have a list of reliable names. The National Solicitors' Network, the Law Society's regional directory or the Council for Licensed Conveyancers can also provide names of people practising in your area.

It makes sense to use a local firm, as they will be aware of local issues, such as planning applications that could affect you. If it's a small firm, make sure they do lots of conveyancing – ask how many conveyances they have dealt with over the past year. As the purchaser's solicitor acts for both the purchaser and the mortgage lender, check that a potential solicitor is on your mortgage lender's 'panel' (i.e. has been approved by them), as this will save the expense and delay of bringing yet another solicitor into the equation.

## Fees

Conveyancing is an area where it is important not to choose on price alone. Most solicitors and conveyancers will give a free quotation over the phone and these may vary a lot. The cheapest might well be the best, or it may be cheap because the firm cuts corners or the work is done by trainees. But high fees are no guarantee either, as solicitors who perceive themselves as high-powered and superior can be impossible to contact and may regard conveyancing as trifling work.

## Internet and telephone conveyancing

There are some very low-cost conveyancing packages to be had via the Internet. These are all provided by qualified practitioners, or the companies wouldn't be allowed to take on the work. Here again, the crucial thing is personal recommendation. These companies are not local, unless you happen to live where they are based, so the whole process is remote, although you are in touch by e-mail, post and phone. Even when you know the name of the person who is supposed to be handling your business, a 'call-centre' attitude often prevails. No one will talk to you until you give a reference number and password, and even then you may be talking to someone who knows nothing about your case apart from what they can see on a screen.

The test of these companies comes when the going gets rough (and by then it's too late for regrets), but if yours is a bog-standard transaction, and someone you trust has found the service satisfactory, telephone or Internet conveyancing can be very good value. One plus point is that you can log into your file at any time to see how things are going.

## Organizing your paperwork

Buying a home involves a lot of paperwork and record-keeping, and there will be countless times when you want to consult a document quickly. The only answer is to create a super-efficient, clearly labelled filing system, into which you will put:

- copies of every letter you send or receive (have separate folders for solicitors' letters, mortgage lenders' letters, estate agents' letters and so on)
- financial records, including a running tally of all the money you spend
- notes of what was said during every meeting or phone conversation
- quotes and estimates for any work on your new property
- everything connected with your mortgage application.

Try to avoid sending handwritten letters as they look less professional than typed ones; and, if you are buying and selling at the same time, remember to keep separate folders for each deal. Boring though it sounds, this system will save you the fury and frustration of scrabbling around for elusive documents when you need them in a hurry, and you will have a permanent record of your house or flat purchase.

## Checking progress

Once conveyancing is in progress, it's up to you to keep chivvying everyone – your solicitor, estate agent, surveyor and mortgage lender – to push the sale through as quickly as possible, so there is no time for anyone to gazump you (see page 104) or back out of the deal.

Whatever kind of conveyancer you use and however conscientious they are, they will be dealing with a lot of other clients at the same time. So, to make things happen as quickly as possible don't just assume everything that can be done is being done. Keep phoning to find out how things are progressing and, if nothing has happened for a while, ask why. It is best to stay on reasonable terms with your conveyancer, though, as if you get stroppy he or she can refuse to go on acting for you!

## Getting a firm mortgage offer

If your mortgage is already arranged in principle, your lender may have given you a mortgage certificate, stating how much they would be prepared to lend you, subject to their valuation of the property you want to buy. If this is still valid (times vary from six weeks to six months), you won't have to fill in yet another form about your income and commitments, though they will need proof of income if you haven't already provided this.

If you haven't arranged a mortgage, waste no time in choosing a suitable lender and mortgage product (see Chapter 3) and completing an application in respect of yourself and the property. Ask how long the lender is likely to take to make an offer and make sure you have the name of the person who is handling your application so you can ring them from time to time to check on progress.

Once the lender has received your application, they will send a surveyor to do a valuation and report on the condition of the property. This is to make sure it's worth at least what you have offered and more than the sum you have asked them to lend you. At this stage you should be able to get the lender to give you a provisional date for when the mortgage will be advanced (i.e. when they will transfer the money to your solicitor, so he can buy the property on your behalf). Your solicitor will not let you exchange contracts until you have a definite mortgage offer.

When the offer comes there will be some conditions. The standard ones say you should:

- keep the home in good repair
- not let all or part of it without their permission
- not make major alterations without their permission
- keep it insured
- inform the lender of any local authority proposals that would affect the property
- not apply for an improvement grant without their permission.

Then there may be some special conditions – for example:

- You must carry out certain repairs within a specified period
- You will not receive the full amount of the loan until certain essential work (such as damp and woodworm treatment) has been completed. This is called a 'retention'.

Read the mortgage offer carefully to make sure the interest rates, terms and conditions are what you expected.

# The survey and valuation report

**Everyone dreads them, especially sellers, but survey reports are essential if you want to avoid nasty surprises after completion.** They give you confidence in your purchase and can save you many times their cost.

## Surveys

Surveys are expensive but useful. Besides telling you whether a property is worth what you are paying, they can warn you of any repairs that are likely to become necessary in your first years of ownership and of any serious defects that might make you reconsider buying the property. If you still want to go ahead despite serious problems, you can use the contents of the survey as solid grounds for renegotiating the purchase price.

Some people assume the mortgage lender's valuation is a comprehensive survey, but it is not – it is simply a superficial report on the condition of the house or flat. If you are a cash buyer (buying without a mortgage), you won't even have the benefit of this basic information, so it is even more important to commission a survey of your own. There are three different types of survey:

- valuation report
- home-buyer's survey and valuation
- structural survey.

Costs vary from about £250 for a valuation report to around £400 for a home-buyer's survey and upwards of £500 for a full structural survey. All mortgage lenders insist on a valuation report, and the surveyor who does this will normally undertake either of the more in-depth inspections for an additional fee. Afterwards, he or she will tell you if any additional inspections – such as timber or damp reports – are necessary.

When Home Information Packs (see page 86) become compulsory there should be no need for buyers to commission their own surveys unless, for any reason, they are not satisfied with the one in the pack. Lenders, too, should not need a further valuation (though some may insist on it) as long as the pack report is by a qualified surveyor – that is to say, a member of Royal Institution of Chartered Surveyors (RICS), the Association of Building Engineers (ABE) or the Architecture and Surveying Institute (ASI). These bodies are responsible for upholding standards in the profession and can give you the names of qualified building surveyors in your area.

Almost all surveys tend to make worrying reading because they mention so many problems – both existing defects and potential ones that might be uncovered by a specialist inspection. And there is the inevitable technical jargon. However, the general summary usually puts all this in perspective by telling you that the property is generally in good condition and worth the price you are paying, or perhaps not in very good condition and priced too high. If in doubt, have an informal chat with the surveyor, who will be able to tell you in plain language what is important and what isn't. Ask whether he recommends you go ahead with the purchase and what any essential repairs are likely to cost.

## Valuation report

This is the one that's required and arranged by your lender, although you pay for it. A valuation report takes into account only basic factors such as a property's location, its age and type, and its general state of repair. As it is not a survey, it doesn't guarantee that the building is structurally sound or that there are no serious defects that will be expensive to put right.

The purpose of the report is to ensure that the property is worth what you have asked to borrow. If you have asked for a high LTV (say 95 or 100 per cent) and the property is valued at less than the purchase price, this could affect the amount of your loan. Mortgage lenders usually let you see the valuation report and, surprisingly, nine out of ten home-buyers are happy to rely on this to satisfy themselves about the condition of their new home.

Occasionally, if a property is in a really bad state, a mortgage lender will withdraw their offer altogether. You can then try another lender, but one of the first questions they will ask is whether anyone else has refused a loan on the property. If you are buying the place to do it up or convert it, there are ways round this, such as a specialist lender or a temporary bank loan, but do make sure there are no redemption penalties as you will want to remortgage as soon as the property is up to scratch.

## Home-buyer's survey and valuation

The home-buyer's survey follows a standard format laid down by the RICS. About ten pages long, it includes:

- an assessment of the general condition and value of the property
- a description of the property and its location (type, age, construction, accommodation, garage, garden)
- an inspection for signs of movement or cracking due to subsidence or defects in the foundations
- timber defects such as woodworm and rot

- dampness (damp-proof course, rising and penetrating damp, condensation)
- insulation (comments on roof and wall insulation, as well as energy conservation)
- an examination of the roof, chimneys, main walls, gutters, downpipes, external joinery and external decoration
- an inspection of the interior (roof space, ceilings, floors, internal walls and partitions, fireplaces, internal joinery and decoration)
- a non-specialist assessment of the services – electricity, gas, water, heating, drainage, boundary walls and fences, and outbuildings
- comments on any legal and other matters (tenure, buildings consents, guarantees).

The report will clearly state which repairs should be remedied 'as soon as possible after purchase' and which should be undertaken 'in the near future'. And there's usually a warning that you should obtain quotes for any urgent repairs before exchanging contracts.

## Structural survey

This is advisable for very old or unusual houses and is sometimes recommended if a home-buyer's report has uncovered potentially serious problems (though in practice it's often best to ditch that house and look for another). A structural survey looks at broadly the same things as a home-buyer's report, but is more detailed and thorough. It should be carried out by a member of the RICS, ABE or ASI.

A surveyor will usually ask if there are any aspects of the property that you feel need a more detailed inspection, so mention anything you may have noticed – ropy-looking plumbing or electrics, damp patches, odd smells, suspicious cracks. And tell him/her about any major works you are planning. For example, if you intend to rewire or replumb you won't need a detailed critique of these services, and if you intend to knock down any walls your surveyor can tell you whether this will be simple or costly. Put any specific requests in writing so you will have some redress if faults appear later.

Surveyors generally cover themselves by stating that certain things (such as floorboards or electrical wiring) could receive only a 'visual inspection', since owners are seldom keen to have skirting boards removed or flooring ripped up. They usually spot things that are visible or measurable, but may miss things that are hidden or depend on circumstances. If it's not raining, for example, a surveyor probably won't notice that a skylight leaks, especially if the owners have carefully camouflaged any telltale signs of this.

# Further reports

Depending on the outcome of the structural survey, you may decide that further, more specialized reports are required.

## Structural engineer's report

If a surveyor has noticed significant structural defects he may suggest a structural engineer's report, to assess whether these represent a risk to the future stability of the building and to advise on any remedial action. Surveyors and structural engineers are very cautious people, so it may not be strictly necessary to undertake all the work they recommend. However, if the same problems crop up in a buyer's survey when you want to sell the property, you may find you can't sell or have to drop the price. So only go ahead if you can afford to rectify the problem or if the house or flat is such a bargain that it is worth the risk.

## Quantity surveyor's report

This is a detailed estimate of the costs involved in extensive building works. It is only necessary if you are planning a major conversion or renovation.

## Timber report

If a surveyor suspects woodworm, wet rot or dry rot, he will recommend that you get a specialist company to assess the extent of the problem. While it is essential to tackle these problems where they exist, remember that it is in the interests of these companies to find work that needs doing. Get at least three estimates, although even then you may well find they don't all agree about what has to be done. Most of the big established companies provide free estimates, but smaller companies tend to charge less for the actual work and offer a more personal service.

## Woodworm

This is often present in older buildings and is easy to spot as the timber is full of tiny holes. Woodworm needs treating unless the owner can supply a written guarantee to show that the work has already been done. If a specialist says it needs treating again, this will be covered by the original guarantee – as long as it's transferable, still valid and the company hasn't gone out of business. Fortunately, woodworm is relatively cheap and easy to treat.

## Wet rot

This can affect any untreated timber that has been exposed to prolonged damp. It particularly affects door and window frames that have not been regularly painted. It's easy to spot as the wood feels soft or damp and bits pull away easily. Wet rot can be easily dealt with by a general builder or specialist timber company.

## Dry rot

Dry rot is a fungus that attacks and breaks down wood, and is the most expensive timber problem to treat. It occurs in timber with a moisture content of over 20 per cent, and when firmly established it looks like a flat white pancake that you can peel away. Dry rot can cross bricks and masonry and, because it often starts in inaccessible places, it may be far advanced by the time it is discovered. It is treated by cutting out and replacing all the affected woodwork and treating the surrounding timbers and masonry with a chemical preventative.

## Rising damp

This is found up to about 1 metre from the ground. Sometimes it is detectable only with a damp-meter, but clear-cut cases are easy to spot as wallpaper starts to peel off and paint begins to blister. Damp that you can't feel and that doesn't show may not be as serious as a specialist company would have you think. If in doubt, keep the room well ventilated and do nothing for the time being. If no obvious damp appears there may well be no problem. Where there is a problem, it is treated by injecting a damp-proof course (DPC) of silicone resin into the wall, hacking off the internal plaster to a height of 1 metre and replacing it with waterproof plaster. Get several quotes as, again, reports and estimates will differ.

## Penetrating damp

This is usually caused by a leaking roof, gutter or window frame. Specialist treatment is not normally necessary. All that's needed is for a builder to find the source of the leak, rectify it and replaster the damp area.

## Recently built houses

All new houses are covered by a ten-year warranty, from either the National House Building Council (NHBC) or the Zurich Municipal Warranty. However, it's worth having a survey done if the warranty is nearing its end, since you should not have to pay for any work covered under the warranty.

# Countdown to exchange of contracts

**'Exchange of contracts' is the legal term for the moment when the contract to buy and sell becomes binding.** Once contracts have been exchanged, the pressure is off and everyone breathes a huge sigh of relief. You now put down a 10 or 5 per cent deposit, which you will forfeit if you fail to complete the deal (you could also be sued for breach of contract). Before exchange of contracts, both buyer and seller are free to change their minds. After exchange, there is no pulling out.

### How it works – or doesn't

Some time before exchange two identical contracts are drawn up, one signed by the buyer, the other by the seller. The two solicitors then hold on to these until all the necessary investigations are complete. When both solicitors and their clients are satisfied that everything is in order, the contracts are swapped, so the buyer's solicitor has the contract signed by the seller and vice versa.

The time delay between the acceptance of an offer and exchanging contracts can cause all sorts of problems. Among the worst are:

- Gazumping – when an unscrupulous seller demands more money or accepts a higher offer just before exchange, leaving the original buyer with a wasted mortgage application and survey fees, and their own purchaser champing at the bit
- Gazundering – when an equally unscrupulous buyer waits until contracts are nearly exchanged and then finds some spurious reason for paying less than the agreed price. By this time, the seller may have proceeded so far along the path of their own purchase that they are forced to accept
- Contract races – when a vendor accepts an offer from two or more would-be buyers, and whoever gets to exchange of contracts first buys the property. Some brave (or foolish) buyers enter knowingly into this race, but most find out only when they are pipped to the post.

The government believes that Home Information Packs will make it much harder for people to play these time- and money-wasting games, because getting searches, surveys and enquiries done before a property goes on the market will enable buyers with no mortgage hold-ups to proceed to exchange within about a fortnight instead of the six to eight weeks it now takes. However, there is still no sure-fire way of avoiding that other great cause of delays: a break in the chain.

### A break in the chain

Sometimes contracts for as many as four or five homes are all due to be exchanged on the same day, to complete a chain. All it takes to wreck everyone's plans is for one of those transactions to be delayed – perhaps because someone's buyer is mucking about or even because one property in the chain still isn't under offer. Everyone has to wait for the missing link to join up or, in a worst-case scenario, go back to square one.

Sometimes in these circumstances a vendor will be so keen not to lose you that they offer to leave your completion date open to allow you time to find another buyer, providing you don't delay the exchange. Don't be tempted by this, however much you want the property you're trying to buy. Even when there's no deadline all sorts of things could happen to make your position impossible – for example, if house prices dropped suddenly you could be left with a serious shortfall.

Although Home Information Packs won't prevent chains being broken, they should make this less common because if people know they are expected to exchange contracts on a purchase within about two weeks, they won't make serious offers on a property for sale until they know they have a rock-solid buyer for theirs.

## Before exchange

There are a number of things that need to happen before an exchange of contracts can go ahead.

Once you have instructed your solicitor to act, he or she will:

1. Ask the seller's solicitor to send a draft contract, and obtain the title deeds to the property. This will be a copy of the entry in the Land Registry or, if the property is unregistered, a copy of the title deeds. Both are absolute proof of the ownership of the property

2. Make sure no one else has a right to any proceeds from the sale of the property, and that there are no loans to be repaid from the proceeds of the sale

3. Check that the property is sold with vacant possession – this ensures that there are no sitting tenants and that the property will be empty and ready for you to occupy on completion day

4. (For leasehold properties) check the terms of the lease to make sure there are no restrictive clauses that limit what you can do with your property, or that would affect its future saleability

5. Obtain answers to a set of standard questions called 'preliminary enquiries' or 'enquiries before contract'. This includes questions about:
   - mains services, boundaries, fences and rights of way, and whether there have been any disputes over these
   - building-regulation certificates, planning consents and any guarantees relating to timber- or damp-treatment, or other work carried out on the property
   - what will be left behind in the way of fixtures and fittings. Normally anything that is part of the fabric of the property, or cannot be removed without causing damage, is included in the sale. But there may be other things that you and the vendor have agreed will be left behind, such as carpets, curtains and blinds, kitchen equipment, light fittings, shelves and fitted gas fires.

   Give your solicitor a list of these items to avoid any disputes later and, when you are sent the completed enquiry form, check that they and anything else you assumed would be left (such as plants, bathroom fittings, sheds or wardrobes) are included. It is not always possible to anticipate what vendors will remove – some even take away the fireplace

6. Undertake local searches to find out if there are any new roads or other developments that would affect your property. This involves sending a standard form to the local authority – who sometimes take an eternity to return it.

   These searches relate mainly to the property itself, so if there is an empty or derelict building near your property call the council's planning department, who should be able to tell you if it's about to spring to life as a round-the-clock lap-dancing club

7. Carry out water searches (a set of standard questions to the local water authority) and any other searches that might be appropriate to the location of the property

8. Agree amendments to the draft contract so it contains everything that has been agreed between buyer and seller, and send it to you to sign (your signature alone is not a legal commitment – that comes when contracts are exchanged)

9. Agree a completion date – usually two to four weeks from exchange of contracts.

## The Law Society TransAction Protocol

Under this voluntary scheme, the seller's solicitor sends the buyer's solicitor an initial package containing:

- the draft contract
- copies of the Land Registry entries or title deeds
- a property information form with answers to preliminary enquiries
- a fixtures, fittings and contents form
- (sometimes) local authority and other searches.

The purpose of the scheme is to get all the paperwork moving as quickly as possible.

Before contracts can be exchanged, your solicitor will also need to know that:

- your survey has been made and accepted
- you have a written mortgage offer (or that funds are available, if you are a cash buyer)
- your deposit is ready.

You should now check that:

- the terms of the contract are as agreed
- your buyer and lender are aware of the completion date
- you can arrange a removal for the agreed date
- you have insured your new home from the date you move in.

## Exchange

Although exchange of contracts involves an actual physical exchange of signed documents and the handing over of your deposit, the precise moment of exchange occurs during a telephone call between the two solicitors or conveyancers, using established procedures laid down by the Law Society. Your solicitor will phone to let you know that this has happened and nothing can now prevent you (or let you off) buying the property. Celebration time!

## After exchange

The time span between exchange and completion can be anything from a few days to a few months, depending on what was agreed in the contract. Normally it's between two and four weeks. While you are busy arranging your move, your solicitor or conveyancer (or you yourself, if you're a DIY conveyancer) will be preparing the transfer document that transfers legal ownership to you, and making sure your mortgage loan is available for the completion date. If you have chosen an endowment mortgage, the life-insurance part must be up and running by the completion date.

If there is anything in the contract about repairs or renovations that the vendor will undertake before completion, make sure these have been carried out because it is very difficult to enforce such things after completion.

## Legal processes between exchange and completion

- The vendor's solicitor sends your solicitor copies of past and present deeds so he/she can make a final check that the person selling the property really owns it.
- Your solicitor prepares a transfer document. This is the deed that passes the vendor's interest in the property to you. If the land is unregistered, a different document called a 'conveyance' is prepared.
- This document is sent for signature by the seller.
- Your solicitor prepares the final mortgage documents. You sign the mortgage deed and your solicitor applies for the mortgage money to be released. It is normally paid by electronic transfer at midday on the day of completion.
- You give your solicitor a cheque for any purchase money that is not coming from your mortgage or sale.
- Your solicitor carries out final searches to make sure there are no undisclosed mortgages or charges on the property, and the vendor is not bankrupt.

## Completion day

- Using the money that you and your lender have provided, your solicitor pays the balance of the purchase price.
- The seller's deeds are handed to your solicitor and any outstanding mortgages on the property are paid off.
- The deeds pass to your mortgage lender as security for the loan, or to you if you have no mortgage.
- The seller moves out – normally by midday – and you are handed the keys.
- You are now the legal owner of the property and you can move in – hurray!

## After completion

Your solicitor:

- advises the lender and any other interested parties (such as the freeholder if it is a leasehold and the life-insurance company if there is an endowment mortgage) that completion has happened
- sends the transfer or conveyance to the Inland Revenue and pays any stamp duty
- registers your title with the Land Registry
- sends you a 'completion statement' giving a financial summary of the whole transaction
- sends you a bill. If there was sufficient money left over after completion, your solicitor will have paid him/herself with it, rather than wait for your cheque.

## If something goes wrong

It's unusual for things to go wrong on or after completion day. Occasionally, however, one of the following might occur:

### The seller has removed things that the contract agreed they would leave behind

First contact the seller to request that the items be returned. They may simply have forgotten, or perhaps the removal men made a mistake. Failing this, your solicitor can make a claim for their return and the cost of reinstalling them. In the last resort, the seller can be sued, although this is expensive unless you do it through the Small Claims Court (claims up to £5,000) and represent yourself

### The seller has left furniture and fittings in the house that the contract agreed would be removed

It's extremely annoying to arrive at your new home, tired and with a vanload of stuff, only to find that it is still full of the previous owner's furniture. This sometimes happens when a property has been let furnished to tenants and hasn't been emptied because the furniture is worthless or the owner can't be bothered. First contact the seller directly or through your solicitor to check that there hasn't been a mistake. If this doesn't prompt instant action, the quickest solution is to ask your removal company (they are used to this) to take the furniture away – usually to a dump. You could try and claim this extra cost back from the seller, though it may be more trouble than it's worth

## The seller fails to move out

If there are any signs that that this might happen, instruct your solicitor to hold up the transfer of your money. He or she will then serve a 'notice to complete', requiring the seller to complete the sale within ten working days. You can claim compensation for the extra costs of delaying your move. If the seller still doesn't move out, you have a right to withdraw from the contract and may be advised to start legal proceedings

## The property turns out to have a serious defect you didn't expect

You can claim against your surveyor if the defect should have shown up in your survey. The problem here, even if you find the roof leaks or there are rotten floorboards under the carpet, is that surveyors always protect themselves by saying there was no access to the roof space or the carpets could not be taken up. But you may have a case if you specifically asked the surveyor to check these things. Negligence is very hard to prove in court, so try the RICS arbitration scheme first.

You may have a claim against the estate agent or the seller under the Property Misdescriptions Act if you feel you were deliberately misinformed. Remember that estate agents always put a disclaimer at the foot of property details. If it is a new property, you can make a claim under the NHBC or Zurich Municipal guarantee

## Problems with lawyers

If you think your lawyer has overcharged you, you can apply to the Law Society for a Remuneration Certificate, which states whether his or her fees are fair and reasonable. If you think your solicitor or conveyancer has been negligent, seek advice from the Office for the Supervision of Solicitors (OSS) or the Council for Licensed Conveyancers (CLC). Both these bodies consider complaints about poor service and conduct, and the OSS can order a refund of fees or compensation. However, if you have suffered financially as a result of legal negligence your claim must be taken to an independent solicitor on the Law Society's 'negligence panel' – your first consultation will be free. Both solicitors and conveyancers are required by law to have negligence insurance.

If you are not satisfied with the way a complaint has been handled, you should contact the Legal Services Ombudsman.

# CONVEYANCING – A CAUTIONARY TALE

**First-time buyers Kate and Julian D obtained several conveyancing quotes for the purchase of their one-bedroom flat in a converted Regency house in Bath. These ranged from £150 to £500 and, since Kate and Julian were already overstretching themselves, they went for the lowest quote. But they lived to regret this because there were a number of problems with the lease and it turned out to be quite a complicated purchase.**

The original solicitor they had spoken to now had bigger fish to fry, so she passed the job to her assistant who was slow and inexperienced. Whenever Kate or Julian rang to ask why things weren't moving more quickly, he insisted it was the other side that was holding things up. But when they contacted their vendor to ask what the problems were, they discovered that the main obstacle was their own solicitor who was taking days to respond to communications. Eventually Kate and Julian demanded that their file be passed to a more experienced conveyancer and this was done – although now they were treated like 'difficult clients' every time they rang the office. To add insult to injury, the final bill after completion day was almost as much as the highest original quote because of all the 'extra work' involved in sorting out the lease.

## Property owners should have wills

Everyone should make a will, but this becomes doubly important once you are a property owner so there are no doubts about what should happen to your estate in the event of your death. If you don't write a will, the government effectively writes one for you. This process takes a long time and your property may not be distributed as you wish – for example, a spouse may receive only half your estate. Some solicitors charge less for a will if they are handling your conveyancing at the same time. If your affairs are simple, you can draw up your own will, providing it is done correctly, or use a professional will writer (there are now also some cheap and efficient online services).

If a will is not drawn up properly it could be invalid, so make sure that any will writer you approach is a member of the Society of Will Writers, the Willwriters' Association or the Institute of Professional Willwriters. Keep your will in a safe place – and tell your executors where it is.

# 6

# Planning removal day

**Congratulations! You've exchanged contracts, and – with luck – everything will be downhill from here.** But don't put your feet up just yet because the next few weeks will be among the busiest of your life.

# Fixing the date

**There's no law that says you have to move into your new home on the day that you complete and, if there is messy building work to be done, it makes sense not to.** But obviously this will depend on whether you have somewhere else to stay and to store your things. Larger removal companies will provide an inclusive quote for moving your stuff out, storing it and moving it to your new home when required. Alternatively, you can store it in the garage or in one room of your new home if either is big enough, but protect everything well because dust gets everywhere once builders move in.

If you are moving on completion day, the date has to be agreed with the people you are buying from and selling to, but make sure it's one that really suits you. Friday is the most popular day, mainly because it's when most completions take place. The chief advantage of a Friday is that it gives you the weekend to settle in and get organized before going back to work on Monday. The disadvantage is that you won't be able to get hold of anyone over the weekend if you need essential services connected, or if something urgently needs delivering or repairing. Removal firms also tend to get very booked up for Fridays, so you'll need to contact them well in advance.

The beginning and end of the month are also popular moving times, so you are most likely to get the removal company of your choice if you opt for midweek and midmonth. The best way to make the whole thing as stress-free as possible is to take two or three days off work and run them into the weekend, so you'll have several days to get sorted – and hopefully some time to rest and enjoy your new home – before returning to work.

# Organizing the removal

**Choosing the right removal company will make all the difference to your move.** Ideally you want people who are careful, efficient, pleasant and not fazed by minor difficulties like a sofa not fitting through a door. There are ways round every practical problem and, with everything else you have to think of on this day, you want to avoid the kind of removal men who get grumpy or make a drama out of a crisis – and over-chatty ones who use the excuse of a cup of tea to tell you their life story.

The costs of the removal will depend on how far away you are moving, how technically difficult the move is (top-floor flats with no lift are not favourites), how much there is to move and whether there any awkward items like giant dressers or pianos (which sometimes need a specialist). A long-distance move may have to be spread over two days, which means paying for overtime and overnight stays.

Get two or three quotes, but don't choose on price alone. The best recommendations come from friends and neighbours, who may also be able to tell you which local firms to avoid. The estate agent you bought from will be able to give you a couple of names (make sure they are not his or her relatives!), and the British Association of Removers (BAR) or the National Guild of Removers and Storers can also supply details of members in your area.

Phone estimates are risky, unless it's a very small move, because someone from the company needs to see your home and contents in order to get a clear idea of the work involved in packing and moving. When the estimator comes, show him or her everything that needs to go, including items in sheds and lofts, but remember also to point out anything that is not being taken. Ask how many men will be provided and how big the van is. Size matters here because your move will take much longer if, as often happens, the men have to deliver one vanload and then go back for another.

Ask what provision is made for clothes. Most removal companies now provide 'wardrobe' packing cases in which clothes can stay on their hangers. Other clothes and linen can normally be left in drawers.

Estimates usually come on a standard form giving the date, the two addresses, and the price and any terms and conditions. Read the small print carefully to make sure there is nothing unacceptable. The estimator will probably not be there on the day you move, so when you accept the estimate put in writing any special instructions you gave him.

## Insurance

Most specialist removal companies have insurance that covers damage to furniture and any items they have packed, but not damage to items they have not packed, so make sure your contents insurance covers possessions in transit. If not, it's worth paying an additional premium for this. There will be exclusion clauses so check what these are. If anything is especially precious or delicate – jewellery, paintings, fragile antiques, computer or audio equipment – it may make sense to pack them separately and transport them carefully in your own car.

## To pack or not to pack

Removal companies usually offer a choice of services:
- They do all your packing and unpacking and take away the cases.
  Pros: the most effortless kind of move – ideal for people who are elderly or unfit, have small children or are just too busy or too lazy to pack.
  Cons: more expensive and you have to be sufficiently on the ball at the end of a tiring day to be able to say where you want everything put – not just your furniture but all your bits and pieces
- They do the packing and you do the unpacking at your leisure.
  Pros: allows you to close the door on the removal men as soon as everything is in the house, and gives you time to think about where you want to put things.
  Cons: unpacking takes a long time and is tiring. You have to dispose of the empty boxes or (if they are returnable) store them until the removal company collects them
- They pack only your crockery and glass, and provide cases for you to pack everything else yourself.
  Pros: takes care of the most fiddly bit of packing, and fragile items are less likely to break if professionally packed (and will be covered by the removers' insurance).
  Cons: you have to pack the contents of bookcases, shelves and cupboards yourself
- They provide the cases and you pack everything yourself.
  Pros: cheaper than all the above, and you know exactly where everything is because you've labelled the cases yourself.
  Cons: takes a long time and is tiring. Don't try to do it all on the night before you move – start well in advance.

## A man with a van

If it's a small move and you're using a man with a van (and a couple of mates), he will not expect to do your packing for you, and will probably not be able to supply you with packing cases. But supermarkets are often happy to give you some of the rigid cardboard crates that their vegetables arrive in. These are an ideal size for things like books and crockery because they are not too heavy when full. A one-man removal business almost certainly won't have any insurance that covers your things.

Pros: cheaper than a removal firm and you're not doing all the heavy lifting yourself.

Cons: the removers will be less experienced at negotiating stairs and doorways, and so more likely to damage your furniture.

## Do-it-yourself

Around 300,000 people a year, many of them first-time buyers, move house without using professional removers. The only costs are the hire of the van, petrol and insurance (which is essential) – or just petrol and insurance if you know someone who can lend you a van. If you're not keen on the idea of driving a large unfamiliar vehicle (most experienced car-drivers adapt very quickly), you can hire a van with a driver, who may or may not be willing to help with loading and carrying. A successful DIY move needs lots of strong helpers.

Self-drive van companies can be found in small ads or the Yellow Pages. Most of the bigger ones will want to know that you have held a driving licence for at least a year and that it is clean. Some also require you to be over 21, although the minimum legal age for driving a small-goods vehicle is 18. If you are moving a long way away, hire the van in the place you are moving to, so you don't have a return drive at the end of the moving day (with someone else coming by car to take you home).

It is hard for an amateur to gauge the right size of van. If it's a local move, it doesn't matter much because you can make two or three journeys, but if you're moving further away, a 7.5-tonne box van (the maximum size you are permitted to drive without an HGV licence) will hold the average contents of a one-bedroom flat, but not of a three-bedroom house. To make loading easier, you ideally need a van with a let-down tailboard or ramp – or, even better, a hydraulic tail lift. Some hire companies do an all-in package that includes van, cardboard packing cases and a trolley to move heavy items.

When stacking a van, make sure everything is wedged very firmly so it doesn't move around in transit, and put plenty of blankets and rugs between surfaces to prevent scratches. Professional removers always load the heaviest things in last, especially if these are going upstairs, so they can deal with them first before they get tired. But for maximum stability, it's also important to distribute the load evenly.

Pros: cheap, and you're in control.

Cons: physically exhausting and it may take several journeys.

## Storage

If you can't move straight from your old home to your new one, you will have to put your furniture and possessions into store. There are three types of storage:

- Depository: your furniture and packing cases are stored loose, but covered, in a space you have rented in a large warehouse. You can inspect them at any time, though there may be a charge for this
- Containers: all your possessions are packed into sealed containers at your home and stored unopened in a warehouse until you need them
- Self-store: you rent a lockable unit in a secure purpose-built warehouse to which you have access whenever the building is open. The monthly rental charge depends on the size of your unit.

The storage firm can arrange insurance, or you can ask your own contents insurers to give you special 'all-risks' cover for the time your goods are in store.

## Getting ready to move

Moving is an exhausting business so the earlier you start sorting and packing your possessions, the better. Buy lots of bin bags and be ruthless about chucking things out – why move with items you don't need or want? If it's going to be a big clear-out – and you have a door that goes on to the street – think about hiring a small skip. This costs about the same as paying a rubbish remover, but the advantage is that it sits there for several days so you can keep throwing things in – and it saves endless journeys to the dump. Alternatively, you can ask for a special council collection (there may be a charge for this).

Go through every cupboard, shed, wardrobe and chest, making piles of:

- things you definitely want to keep
- things you're not sure about
- things you don't want, but someone else might
- things no one on earth would want
- complete rubbish – old magazines, worn-out clothes and shoes, chipped crockery and so on.

Chuck out the complete rubbish without a backward glance. If there's still a load of stuff to dispose of after that, you could consider a garage sale or car-boot sale, which might generate a useful sum to help with your moving costs. Include the things you think no one on earth would want along with the rest because people buy all sorts of improbable things at these sales. But don't include the things you're not sure about yet – you'll probably bin most of these the day before you move. The idea is to arrive at your new home with nothing you don't like or will never use.

Other ways to dispose of unwanted items:

- Advertise useful items in the free-ads section of your local paper
- Give good-quality clothes, china, ornaments and books to a charity shop or jumble sale
- Try second-hand furniture shops or house-clearance dealers, though they won't offer you much money.

## Things to organize

- Your post: for a charge, the Royal Mail will redirect your mail for up to 2 years. You can pick up a form at your post office or call the customer service number: 08457 740 740.
- Change-of-address cards: send these out in plenty of time, making sure they include the date of your move. You can buy them, get them professionally printed, or print them on a computer and stick them on a postcard.
- Utilities: arrange to have gas and utility meters read on the day you leave, or you can give your own readings over the phone. Take a note of the meter readings in your new home as soon as you arrive.
- Council tax: tell the council-tax office when you're moving out and where you are moving to if it's the same tax area.
- Water: tell your company the completion date so they can work out a final bill.
- Telephone: you can usually take your phone number with you if you are moving within the same telephone area. If you're moving to a new number there should be no connection charge as long as you take over the line on the day the previous customer moves out. If you need a new phone line or an old one reconnected, arrange this early as it can take an absurdly long time.
- Milk and newspapers: cancel or redirect.
- Heating and hot water: ask for these to be left on.
- Pets: you may want someone to look after your cat or dog on the day of the move – if so, ask them well in advance. Dogs are not usually traumatized by moving house, but a cat may be. If you don't want to leave your cat with strangers, make it comfortable (with food, drink and a litter tray) in a room where no one will disturb it (perhaps the first room to be

emptied out), and do the same as soon as you bring it to your new home. When all the removal men have gone, let it out to explore the house but make sure there are no open doors or windows. It may creep away and hide for a while, but eventually curiosity will get the better of it. Make sure your cat is wearing a tag that gives your new address and phone number, and don't let it out for at least a week to avoid the risk of it wandering off and getting lost.

- Children: older children enjoy moves and can make themselves useful. Younger ones may find it all a bit disturbing and will undoubtedly get under your feet, so if possible arrange for them to spend the day with close friends or relatives. Have their bed and their favourite toys ready for them when they come home.

- Garden plants: carefully dig up any that you are taking away and plant them in containers. Do this well in advance because it's a messy job and you won't feel like doing it on removal day. Don't water plants in big pots just before the move as just adds to their weight. Plants in flower beds are considered fixtures and fittings, so you should have previously itemized them on the contents form if you want to take them with you.

- Appliances: arrange for the disconnection and reconnection of cooker, washing machine and dishwasher. Some removal firms will connect up washing machines if the correct plumbing-in is already there.

- Guarantees and instructions: ask the seller to explain how all the appliances in your new home work and to leave you any instructions and guarantees.

- New carpets: get these laid before you move in if you possibly can (but not if you are moving builders in or redecorating).

- Packing cases/boxes, strong string and parcel tape, lots of newspaper: make sure you have enough of these. Even if a removal company is doing your packing, there are things you will want to pack yourself.

- Notify all the services you use of your new address and phone number:
  - bank and building society
  - National Insurance and Inland Revenue
  - children's schools
  - doctor, dentist, optician
  - library, clubs and societies
  - insurance companies
  - driving and TV-licensing authorities
  - employers
  - credit-card companies
  - magazine subscriptions and mailing lists.

- Arrange parking for the removal van: if necessary, borrow some cones from the local council.

## The day before

- Draw a rough plan showing where each piece of furniture should go in your new home, so you don't have to think about it each time the removal men ask you where to put something.
- Label packing cases clearly so you can identify their contents.
- Put jewellery, money, chequebooks, passport, keys, essential medicines, important documents and other valuables in a locked briefcase. Keep this in a safe place, ready to take with you in the car.
- Don't let any irreplaceable objects (vital computer disks, the novel you've just written, GCSE projects, rare collections) go by removal van. Transport them yourself.
- Pack an overnight case with dressing gown, slippers, toiletries and a change of clothes.
- Turn the freezer up to high, so the food stays frozen in transit. It should not be more than half full when it is moved. (But don't move a freezer with its contents if the journey is a long one as the food will thaw and become a health hazard.)
- Buy snacks and drinks for moving day.
- Make sure you've got enough cash for last-minute purchases and to tip the removal men.
- Put a list of essential phone numbers (solicitor, estate agent, vendor and purchaser, removal company, van hire, utilities, companies delivering things) in your purse or wallet. Assemble any documents you need to have with you on the day (driving licence, removal contract).
- Keep out your vacuum cleaner and cleaning materials – you may want to give your old home a once-over when it's empty and hoover the new one on arrival. Ideally, arrange for a cleaner to do both.
- Pack a separate box (which you will transport yourself) with all the things you'll need as soon as you arrive at your new home:
  pillows, bedding, towels
  toilet paper
  kitchen towel and bin bags
  toys and games
  kettle, tea, coffee, milk (longlife), sugar
  breakfast cereal
  bottled water and soft drinks
  beer, wine, champagne, corkscrew

snack bars, fruit, tinned soup, tin-opener

light bulbs, matches

basic cutlery and crockery, or plastic plates and cups

paracetamol

rubber gloves, washing-up liquid

basic cleaning/disinfecting materials

saucepan

plugs and adapters

pet food and bowl

first-aid kit

basic tool kit, torch and tape measure.

- Go to bed early.

## On the day

- Have a good breakfast.
- Make sure you haven't left any valuables lying about.
- Before the action starts, take children and/or pets where they are going.
- Put any items you are transporting yourself in a safe place where they won't be gathered up by helpful removers. Clearly label them 'Not to go on van'.
- Check there's nothing left in the loft, sheds and fitted cupboards (if you are using wardrobe cases, the removers will fill these straight from your wardrobe).
- Empty the fridge, dry the inside and put the contents in a cool bag.
- Take meter readings.
- Await confirmation from your solicitor that completion has taken place.
- Take the keys for your old property to the estate agent or landlord.
- Check your old home is empty apart from things you've agreed to leave.
- Collect the keys to new your home from the estate agent.
- Move in, check nothing is left in the van, pay the removers – and tip them (if they deserve it).
- Check that all the services are connected – electricity, gas, water, phone.
- Take meter readings at your new property.
- Collect children and/or pets, leave the unpacking until tomorrow, break open the champagne and order a takeaway.

## Top tip

The secret of a successful move is: lists, lists, lists. Forget information technology – the best way to stay sane is to keep a record of everything connected with the practical side of your move in a school-type exercise book that you can carry with you everywhere. You can stick things in it, its pages are big enough to accommodate long lists and sketches and, if you need to refer to important measurements or find crucial phone numbers while you're out and about, it's all there. The other item to have with you at all times is a small tape-measure – there will be countless occasions when you need to use it.

7

# Making the most of your property

**When you've unpacked and settled in, your thoughts will turn to repairs and improvements.** This can be daunting because, unless you've bought a newly built home or one that's been immaculately maintained by someone with the same taste as you, there's likely to be plenty that needs doing. There'll be work you've got to do, work you ought to do and work you want to do. Surveyors' reports are a help here, as they list urgent repairs and usually indicate what other remedial work should be done in the near future. And of course you will have to do anything that was a condition of your mortgage.

# Immediate jobs

**Whenever you move into a new home, there are always a few things that need sorting out right away.**

During the first few days it makes sense to:

- change the locks on the outer doors as you don't know who might have a set of keys, particularly if it's been rented out in the past
- check that the smoke alarm works
- install fire extinguishers
- identify and deal with obvious dangers such as loose stair carpets or holes in the floor
- ask a qualified electrician to check the wiring, and a qualified plumber and central-heating engineer to check the plumbing and central-heating system (gas and electricity companies will do this)
- make sure there is nothing sharp or splintery in the garden, especially if you have children or pets
- locate important controls like the mains stopcock, the fuse box and the central-heating controls.

After that, you'll want to put up shelves and attend to all the small things that are annoying you – leaking taps, loos that don't flush, cracked windows, faulty radiator controls, doors or windows that don't shut properly, broken hinges or handles.

For minor jobs that don't need a qualified tradesman (or woman), your best bet is an experienced handyman who can turn his hand to anything, charges by the day (plus materials) rather than by the job, and is quick and reliable. Such people are as rare as hen's teeth but worth their weight in gold – and absolutely essential to a new home-owner. If you're new to the district, ask your neighbours if they can recommend someone. Otherwise look in the local small ads, but if someone comes with no personal recommendation ask them to do a smallish job to begin with, so you can assess whether this is Mr or Miss Right.

## Do-it-yourself

When you're short of cash, it's tempting to tackle simple jobs yourself – and if you are confident and experienced, this certainly makes sense. But before getting stuck in:

- Make sure it really will be cheaper in the long run – a professional can buy materials at trade prices and will finish the job to a higher standard
- Only attempt jobs you know you can do safely
- Make sure you can complete the task quickly. Half-finished jobs are an eyesore and builders always charge more when they're asked to repair someone else's work, because they know you are desperate
- Don't tackle anything to do with electricity or gas if you are not qualified
- Hire any professional equipment that might make the job easier and save time.

# Improvements

**The wonderful thing about owning your own home is that you can do whatever you like to it – subject, of course, to planning permission and the rules that protect listed buildings.** You can modernize, extend, knock down walls, landscape the garden, or make a cellar- or loft-room. You can go for the minimalist look with bare boards, white walls and one twig in a vase, or fill every swagged and textured square metre with chintz and cheerful clutter. Like your clothes, your home reflects you – your personality, lifestyle, taste and imagination.

But there's more to home-ownership than just creating an environment that suits you. Everything you do to your property, inside and out, will affect its desirability and value when you decide to sell. So every decision you make, from your choice of location, architectural style and decor to the way you maintain and improve your property, can make all the difference between a handsome profit or being lumbered with a white elephant.

This doesn't mean that wacky design ideas are out of the question, but you do need to think carefully about the effect on prospective purchasers before, for example, knocking everything into one massive, galleried living area or creating a *Star Wars* theme home. Unless, of course, you're going to stay in the property until they carry you out.

## Plan it carefully

Before you launch into any major or minor improvements draw up a list of everything you plan to do, so you can make sure jobs are done in the right order. Work that will disturb the plaster and skirtings, such as new wiring and plumbing, should be completed before decoration. Carpets should be put down only when all the messy jobs are finished.

Few people can afford to do everything at once, so you will have to prioritize. If there's a big disruptive job that you're not going to start for a year or so, decisions will have to be made about whether it's worth making small improvements in the meantime. What's the point of replacing that horrendous kitchen floor if you intend eventually to knock down a wall and make an entirely new kitchen–diner? The answer will depend entirely on how much you hate the offending floor and how much some inexpensive vinyl flooring, say, would cost.

## Major work

There are those who say that you shouldn't make any decisions about what you want to do to a home until you've lived in it for a while, and there's probably some truth in this as it does take time to get the feel of a place and understand the way its layout affects your lifestyle. Nevertheless, many new home-owners know exactly what they want to do from day one – perhaps even from their first viewing – and are keen to get on with it.

Major structural work should ideally be done when you are not in residence. If you intend to do it at once and the property is empty, the sellers may allow you to move your builders in between exchange and completion. In that case it may be worth delaying completion on the property you are selling (as long as you've exchanged contracts) and getting a short-term bridging loan, so the messiest work can be done before you move in. Some sellers don't like the idea of structural work being done before completion (in case you can't complete the sale for some reason, and they are left with a building site) but are happy to let you install smaller things like shelves and fitted cupboards.

However, most previous owners only leave on the day you arrive so, unless you have somewhere else to stay, you will have to share your home with workmen – the well-trodden path to a nervous breakdown.

## Is it worth it?

The two most common reasons people give for turning their home into a building site are that the living space is too small or the wrong shape, or they want to increase the value of the property. But structural work, such as building extensions and knocking down walls, brings a lot of dirt and disruption into your life, so you have to be sure it is worth the trouble.

Not everything you do to your home will increase its value. You might think that installing a gym or a jacuzzi would make a property irresistible to future owners, but this is not the case. Even swimming pools put off more buyers than they attract, unless the house is in an area where people expect such things – and have nannies to stop the children falling in.

Here are some other costly items that won't improve the value of your property:

- landscaping the garden – nice, but won't add a bean
- stone cladding – very unpopular, avoid at all costs
- marble bathrooms, gold taps – very 1980s, now naff
- a carport – never looks nice
- a pillared porch – only looks good on a stately home
- modern windows in an old house – never look right.

Good ideas include:

- hardstanding for a car
- a garage
- a conservatory, but only if the workmanship is first class
- home security
- smart kitchens (but only if the old one needs replacing anyway)
- new bathrooms, as long as they're white
- power showers
- open-plan kitchen–diners
- stylish loft conversions (but not poky attics approached by dodgy ladders)
- high-quality double-glazing, especially on busy roads or in exposed locations
- loft and cavity-wall insulation, because it's energy-conscious
- extra loos – always a good idea
- en-suite bathrooms (but not if it makes a bedroom too small).

Structural improvements should not only add value to your home, but also make it a better living space for you. So you need to weigh the upheaval and expense of building works against the investment value and the improvement to your quality of life. Remember that big changes are irrevocable. Once the work has been done, there's no going back.

If you simply want to increase the value of your home (perhaps with a view to selling in the near future), you need to do your maths before launching into costly improvements, because you don't always gain as much as you've spent. For example, if a house or flat already has a modern, serviceable fitted kitchen, fitting an expensive new one won't make it worth any more, and your choice may not be to someone else's taste. If your kitchen is basically OK but not what you'd choose, consider giving it a facelift with new doors, worktops and tiles. On the other hand, extending or knocking down a wall to turn a tiny kitchen into an attractive kitchen–diner is probably a good investment, because well-designed kitchens you can eat in are extremely popular.

Think carefully before combining other rooms. The value of a property depends more on the number of rooms than on the size of them. Some people knock two reception rooms into one because they feel a through room is better for entertaining. Yet they only have a party once a year, and the rest of the time would find life better with a separate dining room and sitting room because they can be used for different activities at the same time – for example, if one person wants to watch TV or chat to a friend, while the other wants to play music or work. With bedrooms, it's almost never a good idea to knock two into one as this will reduce the value of the property. A bedroom is a bedroom, even if there's only room for a cot and a chest of drawers.

So unless you intend staying in a house or flat so long that cost-effectiveness doesn't matter, make sure any improvements you make are in proportion to the value of the property. If you spend £40,000 on a £160,000 house, you probably won't get your money back, whereas the same amount on a house worth £300,000 could be money well spent.

## Extensions

If you've lived in your home for some time and need more space, then extending is a sensible alternative to moving. It may also be more cost-effective, because moving is such an expensive business. But don't expect an extension to make your property worth much more than all the others in the street. Every area has its price ceiling. An extension is only worth considering if there's somewhere you can extend into without spoiling anything else, and its design should always be in keeping with the style of the house.

An extension over a garage is a good way to create an additional bedroom. Or you could kill two birds with one stone by creating a two-storey back extension, giving you more living space downstairs and an extra bedroom or bathroom upstairs. But there's no point if it takes light away from other rooms, or if the new upstairs room is off an existing bedroom (unless you've planned it as an en-suite bathroom).

There are DIY extension kits for single-storey extensions, but the designs tend to be plain (not to say unattractive) and limited. If the new extension is going to take up half a small garden, forget it. Most people would value the garden space more than the extra indoor space.

## Loft extensions/conversions

With lofts, everything depends on the shape of the roof (some lofts just can't be converted), the strength of the floor and what the room will be used for. You may have to move water tanks, and, if you're using the room as a bedroom, it must comply with fire regulations.

The simplest and cheapest way to convert a loft into, say, a playroom or teenage bedroom is to install roof lights (flush, sloping windows) in the existing roof, put in a floor, plaster the walls and install proper stairs (retractable loft ladders are only suitable for occasional use). This can be done for just a few thousand pounds, but is only worth the trouble if the loft is big enough to allow plenty of headroom before it slopes down to the eaves. Lofts without the regulation head height can officially be used only as storerooms.

Adding dormer windows, which jut out from the roof and have their own ceiling, creates more space but is expensive. Bigger dormer extensions (usually permitted only at the back of a property) are more expensive still, but make lovely light rooms. The positioning of the staircase is crucial. If it cuts into a first-floor room that is already small, or makes the landing feel cramped, it may spoil the look of a house. Obviously, the better the conversion and the more versatile the room, the more it will add to the value of the property.

## Conservatories

These are very popular as they provide lovely, light living space and bring the garden into the house. Choose a design that complements the house – most ready-made designs are only suitable for modern houses. Individually designed conservatories by architects or specialist conservatory companies cost more but can look stunning, especially when filled with exotic plants and elegant furniture. First-floor conservatories are also attractive. Heating and ventilation are essential as garden rooms tend to get hot in summer and cold in winter.

## Knocking down walls

There was a fashion, not so long ago, for knocking the hall into the living room, to make one big open-plan space. But halls are more appreciated now – and rooms need doors (unless the house has only one occupant).

As already mentioned, creating a big kitchen–diner out of two smaller back rooms is a very good idea, but it needs to be self-contained. Don't be tempted to incorporate the kitchen into your main living area because you won't be able to shut out the smell and mess of cooking.

If you're determined to knock down a wall to make a through living-room, installing good-quality double doors between the two rooms would make the space more flexible.

## Cellar conversions

Many older properties still have their original cellars, traditionally used for storage. Unlike basements, these don't usually give on to a front or back area and may have little or no natural light, unless there are pavement windows or a coal chute. They may also be damp and badly ventilated but, properly converted, they make good hobby rooms, home offices or teenage dens – and converting a cellar (there are now quite a few specialist cellar companies) is much cheaper than building an extension. You have to bear in mind the following:

- The walls and floor need to be damp-proofed or 'tanked'
- Access should be by a permanent, safe, well-lit staircase
- If there's no natural ventilation, an extractor fan should be installed
- If the central heating can't be extended, individual electric – not gas – heaters should be used.

# Financing and organizing home improvements

**If you have immediate improvements in mind, include the cost of them in your mortgage, as this is the cheapest form of borrowing.** Otherwise, the cheapest way to finance improvements is to increase your mortgage – or remortgage, if you can get a better deal from another lender. But you will need the income to support more borrowing and sufficient equity in the property. However keen you are to perfect your home, it's unwise to overstretch yourself.

If you don't need to borrow much and you want to pay off the loan more quickly, you could consider a personal loan secured on your property (a 'charge'), but the interest will be higher and you will still have to pay for a new valuation. An unsecured personal loan doesn't involve a valuation fee, but this is the most expensive type, with interest rates around twice those of mortgages. Shop around – and check out what your own bank has to offer.

## Do I need an architect?

This depends on what kind of work you are doing. Extensions certainly need some preliminary advice, although if they are simple it may be enough to consult a building surveyor. If possible, use the surveyor who did your home-buyer's report or structural survey as he will be familiar with the building. Both architects and surveyors can help with planning applications, prepare drawings and organize builders. In general, an architect is the best person to consult for work that requires design skills, like new extensions or changing layouts, while building surveyors can help with repairs and renovation.

Consulting an architect or surveyor does not commit you to a long-term contract. You can simply ask their advice about possible ideas (fees for this are charged at an hourly rate) or consult them at specific points during the work. If you ask them to oversee the whole project through from start to finish, they will charge a percentage of the total cost. In theory, having someone else to deal with your builders will save you a lot of hassle – although some builders have no more respect for professionals than they do for customers!

## Choosing a builder

There are three ways to choose a builder – personal recommendation, personal recommendation and personal recommendation. Anything else is a gamble. If an architect or surveyor suggests a builder, they have probably worked with him before and think his work is good, clean, reliable and reasonably priced. Even so, builders can change. For example, if yours is overstretched and decides to use agency labour instead of their own team, you could end up with slow, inconsiderate, messy – even incompetent – workmen in your home.

- If possible, use a builder who has been recommended by a friend or neighbour, and look at their work before making a decision.
- If there's some building work going on nearby, ask the owners whether they would recommend the builder. Find out whether they are: delighted, generally happy, not sure or just plain tearing their hair out.
- Ask your estate agent to recommend a builder (they will probably suggest someone expensive but thoroughly professional). Again, look at their work.
- The Federation of Master Builders (FMB) and the National Federation of Builders (NFB) can supply names of reputable builders in your area.
- Your building and contents policy insurers may have some recommended names in your area.
- Never use a firm that knocks on your door – this tactic is usually a prelude to various scams.

## Employing a builder

Once you have a list of names, how do you choose the 'right' one? And once you've chosen someone, how to you get the work you want done on time?

- Get two or three quotes. This is important even if you know who you want to use, as you'll get an idea of what different people think the job is worth and it may give you some bargaining power.
- Write down everything you want done and include as much detail as possible so you get an all-inclusive quote. If you keep thinking of things while the work is in progress, they will be charged as 'extras'. There are builders who will charge extra for attaching a towel rail to the wall, because the specification for installing your new bathroom didn't include 'fit towel rail', so try to mention everything.
- Make sure you get a written quotation that specifies what work will be done.
- Find out whether the builder is a member of a trade body, such as the FNB, NFB or the Construction Confederation.
- Ask if the work is guaranteed and whether the guarantee is backed up by an insurance policy (in case the builder goes out of business).
- Before signing a contract, make sure everything you specified is there, and add anything that should have been included.
- Establish the order in which the work will be done, and make sure each stage is finished before the next one starts.

- Remember that items like kitchen fittings have long delivery periods, so you may have to order them several weeks in advance.
- Agree a precise date on which work will start and ask for a realistic estimate of when it will end. It's a good idea to give builders an event-related deadline – your parents are coming to stay from Australia, you're having a baby or the Queen is coming to tea – so the work must be finished by that date.

## Payment

Building work is normally paid for at the end of previously agreed stages. Never let yourself be persuaded to pay out more money up front, whatever the excuse, and make the final payment only when all the work has been completed to your satisfaction. It's usual to hold back a proportion of the final payment for four to six weeks, to ensure that the builder will come back if there are problems, but you should notify them in advance if you intend to do this. Always obtain receipts for payments, especially if they are in cash.

## Keeping tabs on progress

It's easy to feel powerless when your home is full of dust, rubble and labourers. But it's your home and you are the employer, so don't hesitate to complain loudly if:
- not enough progress is being made (this can often happen if you are out at work during the day)
- any work has not been done in the agreed way or to an acceptable standard
- there are not enough workers on the job
- they don't turn up, arrive too late or leave too early
- any of your furniture or possessions have been damaged
- things are not tidied up at the end of the day
- the builders' radio or other noise is disturbing you – or your neighbours.

And be sceptical about excuses like 'the van broke down' or 'I ordered it but when I got there they didn't have it'.

Although there are a lot of horror stories (one in five customers swear they will never let builders in their house again!) the vast majority of people end up reasonably (or even perfectly) satisfied with their builders and very glad they had the work done.

# Planning permission and building regulations

**One or both of these is likely to apply if you are considering structural alterations.** The following information is a brief summary, but most councils can supply free planning- and building-regulation booklets.

## Planning permission

The planning system exists to make sure any changes fit in with the surrounding area and do not adversely affect your neighbours. Planning applications are controlled by the local council, and the rules vary according to whether a house is listed or in a conservation area. Generally speaking, you need planning permission if:

- you want to build an extension that:
    - is more than 50 cubic metres or 10 per cent of the original volume of a terraced house, or
    - is more than 70 cubic metres or 15 per cent of the original volume of any other type of house, or
    - would increase the volume of a house by more than 115 cubic metres
- you want to make any alterations to a flat or maisonette that affect the external appearance of the building
- you want to divide off part of your house for use as a separate home
- you want to divide your home for business or commercial use
- you want a loft extension that changes the height or shape of a roof
- you are planning any outbuildings, such as sheds and greenhouses, that are nearer the public road than your house
- you are adding a porch with a ground area of more than 3 square metres.

In conservation and some other areas you may also need approval to:

- put any kind of cladding on the outside of a building
- demolish a building of more than 115 cubic metres
- demolish gates or fences that are next to public land
- take down trees
- put up any fence or building that would obstruct a public right of way
- proceed with any development that would affect protected wildlife species.

You don't normally need planning permission for internal patios, sheds, greenhouses, hardstanding, ponds, swimming pools and even tennis courts, as long as the development:

- is less than 3 metres high
- is not nearer the public highway than your house
- doesn't take up more than half the area of your land
- is purely for domestic use.

Replacement windows and roofs, painting, decorating and roof lights don't need planning permission, but may need listed-building consent or approval from the leaseholder (if your property is not a freehold). Planning rules are complicated, so always check with your local council's planning department before starting work on a project. The council has the authority to make you take down or reinstate any structures that have been changed without planning permission.

When applying for planning permission:

- Discuss your plans with your neighbours to see if they have any comments. In any case, the council will notify them of your application
- Discuss your needs with the planning office before submitting a formal application. They can probably tell you if it is likely to be approved
- Obtain detailed drawings to submit with your application.

Councils have to make a decision on an application within eight weeks, and if permission is refused they must tell you why and whether changing your plans would make a difference. Appeals can be made to the Planning Inspectorate in Bristol, Cardiff or Edinburgh.

## Building regulations

These are completely separate from planning permission and are almost always required when external or internal structural changes are made. Building regulations lay down minimum standards for building materials, sewers and drainage, fire precautions and health and safety, and they apply to new buildings, extensions and alterations. But they are not required if the work is not structural – for example, if you are simply installing new bathrooms and kitchens or new central-heating systems.

# Doing up a wreck

**Renovation is all about bringing a neglected building back to life – and it involves a massive amount of work.** Once the project is finished, however, you will have acquired an attractive and unusual home for about 70 per cent of the price of buying it ready-converted. Very satisfying – although the Americans call this increased value 'sweat equity', on account of all the blood, sweat and tears you have invested.

But it's vital to get your finances right, as you won't end up with a bargain if you pay too much for your wreck in the first place. The rule of thumb for making an offer on this kind of property is first to find out what it will be worth when finished. Then calculate what the work will cost (don't underestimate – renovations always cost about 25 per cent more than you think) and add this to the purchase price. The offer you make should be no more than halfway between the property's final value and what it will have cost you. If you are going to have to rent temporary accommodation while the work is in progress, include that in the costs.

Old barns are particularly sought after because they offer wonderful scope for imaginative interiors. But they have become so popular in recent years that, except in remote areas, there aren't too many unconverted ones left. Other agricultural buildings offer possibilities, as do old schoolhouses, oast houses, windmills, disused churches – in fact, any lovely old place that has been allowed to sink into disrepair. Remember that if a farm building is really remote, you may have to pay to bring in power and water. And always discuss your intended purchase with the local planning department first, as all sorts of rules apply to former farm buildings and you may find you can't install windows – or even create a first floor.

If it's a complete renovation, you will almost certainly need an architect. Choose one who has plenty of experience of conversions, is sympathetic to your ideas and has plenty of his or her own. Look at some examples of their work and ask them to point out features that were their suggestion.

When you've established what you're going to do, your architect will submit your plans to the local authority for planning permission and building-regulations approval. Once you have all the permissions you need, the architect will ask two or three builders he or she knows and trusts to tender for the job.

If your wreck requires only repairs and modernization but not complete renovation, a building surveyor or just a very good builder may be all you need – especially if you already have a clear idea of what you want to do. Remember that if you're not using an architect or surveyor you will have to supervise the work yourself, which involves spending a great deal of time on site and making endless decisions.

One of the joys of doing up a wreck is that you can organize the internal space to your own requirements. Before you go wild, though, bear in mind that:

- moving load-bearing walls is expensive as the floor above has to be supported by a metal beam
- moving kitchens and bathrooms (or installing completely new ones) involves moving drains – also very expensive
- new materials don't work well in old houses, so you will need to hunt down old windows and doors, and reclaimed timber and old bricks
- kitchen and bathroom design should reflect or complement the architectural style
- decoration and furnishings have to be in tune with the rest of the property.

Two phrases beloved of estate agents are 'lovingly restored' and 'many period features' so, wherever possible, restore original attributes. Modern 'maintenance-free' windows, frosted glass and tacked-on porches spoil the look of an old house, as does painting the front elevation a startling colour. For the costs of installing new plastic windows, you could have wooden ones maintained every year for 30 years.

## First things first

The most important jobs are those that make the house dry and structurally secure, so start on the outside and work inwards. Your top priorities are:

- the roof
- chimney and flashings
- gutters and eaves
- external walls
- doors and windows
- damp-proof course
- woodworm, rot and timber treatments.

Once you've got a sound 'shell' (and if there's any money left) you can move on to:

- interior walls, floor, staircases
- rewiring and replumbing

- central heating
- kitchen and bathroom
- carpentry and decoration.

Few people can afford to stay in their old home while restoring a new one so, if the project is going to take several months, try to make one small area of the building dry, warm and habitable first (with a shower, kitchenette and loo), so you can live there while the rest of the work is being done. This will save having to rent a place and enables you to keep an eye on the site and the work.

## Renovation grants

If you own a property that needs major repairs, you can sometimes get help from your local council to meet all or part of the cost of the work. Before applying for a grant, establish exactly what needs to be done and how much it is likely to cost. Councils normally require two written quotes from reputable builders to back up the estimate on a grant application. All renovation grants are means-tested and you will be told how much, if anything, you must contribute yourself. Grants are awarded at the discretion of the local authority, so don't automatically assume you will get one.

Renovation grants may be available for the following:
- to make a dwelling fit (meet health and safety standards)
- to put a dwelling in reasonable repair – this could include a damp-proof course, timber treatment, electrical wiring, defective guttering, repairs to roofs, timbers, walls and foundations, floors, staircases or plaster
- home insulation, such as loft, water tank, pipe and cavity-wall insulation
- heating
- to provide satisfactory internal arrangements – for example, to move a bathroom that is accessible only through a bedroom, or to alter a low doorway or steep staircase
- for works to convert a house into self-contained flats
- to repair the common parts of a building that includes self-contained flats (these can be occupied by tenants or long-leaseholders).

Work is not eligible for a grant if:
- the property was built or converted less than ten years ago
- the property is a second home
- the work is non-essential – i.e. decoration or extensions.

Owner-occupiers have to certify that they or members of their family will occupy the dwelling for the next five years, and landlords must guarantee that they will let the dwelling as a home to someone unconnected to them. Owner-occupiers should usually have lived in the dwelling for the preceding three years, but this condition is sometimes waived so it's worth applying even if you've just moved in.

A free booklet, Housing Renovation Grants, is available from the Office of the Deputy Prime Minister, ODPM Free Literature, PO Box 236, Wetherby LS23 7NB (tel: 0870 122 6236).

Some renovations are eligible for VAT relief on materials, although this depends on the type of building and how long it has been empty; and if really old or interesting listed buildings are considered to be 'at risk', they may be eligible for special grants from English Heritage, but you will have to comply with a lot of regulations and conditions.

## Renovation and self-build mortgages

There are very few specific 'renovation' mortgages, but lenders have at least begun to recognize that renovation and (especially) self-build are a growing area of the market. The average self-builder or renovator is sitting on a property that is worth 20–30 per cent more than it cost them as soon as their building project is finished, so they are, in fact, less of a lending risk than conventional borrowers who may have only a 5 per cent equity in their home. But renovation mortgages are still harder to come by than ordinary ones, although those that exist are just a standard mortgage with special conditions attached.

Once a lender has agreed to lend you the money to renovate, the funds are usually released in three to six stages, depending on how much work there is to do. Normally each instalment is released after the work it relates to has been done, and some lenders won't release the first stage until quite a substantial amount of the project has been completed. Just one product – the Accelerator mortgage (offered by three or four lenders) – releases the money for each stage up front. As with any other mortgage, it pays to shop around as rates vary from lender to lender. Most charge a higher rate of interest until your renovation is complete.

## RENOVATION – CASE STUDY

**In 1997, Marcus and Donna K bought a disused farmyard with an old Kent barn and several modern agricultural buildings. Their original plan was to convert the barn, which was nearly falling down, into a spacious home for themselves and their four young children. However, the local planning department insisted that the barn could not be divided into separate rooms or have a first floor (or any new windows) because the space had to remain 'one void'.**

Nothing could budge them, even though the barn would have collapsed if Marcus and Donna hadn't rescued it, so in the end they put their bedrooms, bathrooms, kitchen and dining room in the attached outbuildings and turned the barn into one enormous living room, the size of a tennis court. Although it took three years for the planning issues to be sorted out, the building work itself (which was achieved with the help of an Accelerator mortgage) was completed in two years.

The family finally moved into their new home in December 2002, after two years in a mobile home on the site. Though disappointed at the way their restoration plans were blocked at every turn, Marcus and Donna now have a unique family home that's already worth 40 per cent more than it cost them.

# Regular maintenance

**It's astonishing how many people spend a small fortune on interior decoration, but don't bother to maintain the outside of their home.** As a result, water comes in and not only wrecks the beautiful decorations but means costly external repairs. Bear in mind that when it comes to selling your property, your buyer's surveyor will be far more impressed by good maintenance than by superficial frills.

The secret of successful property maintenance is 'little and often', as the longer you leave any problem the more expensive it will be to put right. It's better to rub down and repaint window sills every couple of years than have to replace rotten ones after five or six years.

If you are good enough at DIY to do straightforward maintenance jobs yourself, remember they should always be done to professional standards. Amateurish repairs can devalue your property and give future buyers an excuse to knock the price down. If in doubt, consult one of the many excellent DIY manuals on the market.

It's a good idea to go outside and look at your property in the rain from time to time. Persistent drips or overflows may mean a blocked gutter (often just caused by leaves), which can also lead to damp patches indoors. If you can see there's a problem, inside or out, but are not sure what's causing it, get at least two expert opinions (and quotes) before paying someone to repair it.

Interiors must of course be cared for, too. Keep on top of internal decoration and repairs by redecorating and fixing problems as soon as the need is there. When jobs mount up they become daunting – and then you won't want to start them at all.

Regular maintenance, dear home-owner, is the best investment you can make in your property.

# Making money from property

**Recent dramatic rises in property values have encouraged a lot of people to treat property purely as an investment.** But this is an area in which you really need to know what you are doing because, despite the success stories you see on TV, making money from property is not a pushover.

The various options include:
- buying to let – buying and doing up a property that you can let to tenants (furnished or unfurnished) on a long- or short-term basis
- the property ladder – buying a home to do up quickly and sell on for a profit
- property development – buying, doing up and selling properties you never live in.

When people come a cropper it's usually because they have bought in the wrong location, made the wrong improvements or simply spent far too much. When buying property to let or sell on, there are three golden rules:
1. When choosing: steer well clear of properties with drawbacks that you can't put right, such as bad surroundings, traffic noise or dark rooms
2. When budgeting: be realistic about costs and resist non-essential features that will eat into your potential profit
3. When improving: remember that everything you do must appeal to your target market. You are not going to live in this home, so it doesn't have to express your individual creativity.

If you stick to these rules, you will find that turning an undesirable residence into a desirable one can be a profitable enterprise. But bear in mind that if interest rates rocket or prices plummet, a tidy profit can quickly become a massive loss.

## Buying to let
Before starting to look for a rental property, identify your target tenants. All tenants want to live in a reasonably quiet location that's near to shops and transport, but other requirements will depend on their reasons for renting.
- Corporate tenants (business people working temporarily in the area) – can afford high rents because these are usually paid by the company, but they expect a high standard of decor, fixtures and fittings. They look for properties in good areas near their work and usually want two or more bedrooms.

- Young couples – this is a big area of the market because so many couples have to rent a home until they can get a foot on the property ladder. Most young couples want clean, neat, one-bedroom flats with modern kitchens and bathrooms.
- Mobile workers – people whose jobs mean they have to relocate frequently often prefer to rent. Some buy a property as an investment to let out, but live in rented accommodation so they can stay mobile and flexible.
- Sharers – often young professionals or college leavers who have just left home. They want a big living room for shared activities, but don't usually demand or expect superb kitchens, bathrooms and decor.
- Students – not too fussy about the standard of accommodation as long as it's cheap and cheerful and meets health and safety requirements, but they are not the most careful tenants. Student lets must always be furnished.

Once you've identified where you want to buy a property and who you want to let it to, talk to a local letting agent, who will be able to tell you which kinds of properties are most lettable. Make sure there is a real demand for the type of accommodation you will be providing. Newly built properties are usually easy to let as they are very popular with young couples, but you'll probably make more profit from buying a run-down flat and doing it up to a high standard.

### Finding reliable tenants

Advertising in a local paper or shop windows will save having to pay commission to a letting agent, but you'll have no one but yourself to blame if you choose the tenant from hell. When letting without an agent, make sure:

- you have references from any potential tenant's employer, bank and previous landlord
- you and your tenant have both signed a standard 6- or 12-month shorthold tenancy agreement in the presence of an independent witness
- a standing order has been set up for the monthly payments
- any cheque for the first month's rent and deposit (usually six to eight weeks' rent) has been cleared before the tenant moves in. If they're in a hurry, ask for cash
- you make an inventory of all the contents of the house or flat, to be signed by both you and the tenant.

### Letting agents

Most agents offer a choice of three services:

- Introduction: they find a tenant and check references – then all responsibility reverts to you. The charge is normally about 10 per cent of the annual rent

- Introduction and rent collection: the agent collects the rent and is the tenant's first point of contact regarding problems, but you sort out any repairs yourself. This costs about 12.5 per cent of the annual rent
- Full management service: the agent finds a tenant, collects the rent, deals with repairs and deducts the cost of these from your rent cheque. This costs around 15 per cent of the annual rent.

## Doing your sums

Investors in property look for two types of return – income from rent, and capital growth from increases in value. Both these gains are taxed when a property is not your principal residence: you pay income tax on the rental, and capital-gains tax on the capital growth when you sell. But your costs and expenses can be offset against both of these.

Ideally, you should look for a 10 per cent gross annual yield from a property, before expenses. So if the house or flat has cost you £100,000 (made up of the purchase price, stamp duty, renovation and any other costs) the rental income should be about £10,000 a year. The net yield, or profit, will depend on the size of your mortgage repayments, service charges, ground rent and so on.

When deciding how much they are prepared to lend on a rental property, a mortgage lender will be more interested in the projected rental income than your salary. They normally require your income from the property to be between 125 per cent and 140 per cent of your monthly repayments.

## Getting the decor right

All professional lets must offer a high standard of fixtures and fittings, be easy to live in and appeal to a broad range of tastes. As mentioned earlier, corporate tenants, especially, expect contemporary style and a certain amount of luxury. Follow these ground rules:

- Stick to neutral colours everywhere
- Beware of cream or white carpets as they show every mark. Seagrass or sisal solves the problem in living areas. Bedrooms need soft carpets or floorboards with thick rugs
- Use contemporary lighting schemes – wall lights and uplighters rather than ceiling pendants
- Create lots of storage space
- Choose tough, modern furniture with clean lines – again, avoid white or cream. Close-fitting loose covers are ideal; have two sets made, so you can change them quickly for new tenants
- Kitchens need to be bright, light, modern and very well equipped, and should, if possible, have an eating area

- Bathrooms – white suites, a tile or laminate floor, high-quality, unfussy tiling and, if possible, a power shower in addition to a bath
- Patios and gardens should be easy-care. Go for paving, decking and pots.

If you're letting to students keep everything hard-wearing and easy to clean. A low standard of decor will only encourage the occupants not to look after the place. Paint everything white, strip the floors (they can add their own rugs and throws), put washable covers (dark colours) on upholstered furniture and lay tough flooring in the kitchen and bathroom. Keep fixtures, fittings and furniture in a good state of repair, but don't spend a fortune on these as you may have to replace them.

### Safety

Remember that every rental property must have:
- smoke detectors
- fire-retardant upholstery, soft furnishings and bedding
- a gas safety certificate
- regular checks on electrical equipment.

## LETTING – A CAUTIONARY TALE

**Magda H, a young teacher, bought a one-bedroom flat in Reigate, Surrey. A year later she moved to a new job in south London and, as she couldn't afford to buy there, decided to let her Reigate property and use the rent to pay her mortgage while sharing with a friend in London.**

The only flat-seeker to reply to her classified ad was a seemingly nice lady who, unfortunately, didn't have a landlord's reference because she was newly divorced and had just left the marital home. She also had no employer's reference as she had just started a new job. But term was starting and Magda was desperate to get a tenant installed. She also felt quite sorry for this lady, so she gave her the benefit of the doubt.

This 'nice' tenant stopped paying rent after two months, ignored phone calls, letters and visits, and refused to vacate the flat. When she was finally evicted six months later she did a disappearing act without repaying a penny of her rent debt (despite a court order), leaving Magda £3,000 in debt.

## Selling on

Whether you're doing up a place to live in it first and then sell it on, or to sell it on immediately, the critical thing is to make it appeal to the broadest possible cross-section of your target market. So forget your own likes and dislikes and keep a constant eye on your budget.

### Kitchens

A magnificent kitchen can sell a property. The essentials are:

- good-quality fitted units. Kitchen fashions change quickly, so be careful not to spend thousands of pounds on 'yesterday's kitchen'. White, pale cream or a light wood are safer than colour-dragged pine or stainless steel
- lots of workspace and a labour-saving layout
- a separate eating area – if possible opening on to a garden or patio
- high-quality fitted appliances
- good lighting, especially over work surfaces
- a tough, attractive floor – high-quality vinyl, wood laminate or (top favourite) Mediterranean-style ceramic tiles.

### Bathrooms

- If there's only one (in a house) it must be upstairs.
- Plain white sanitaryware looks like it's staying in fashion so, if you're ripping out an old coloured suite, replace it with a white one.
- Choose fresh-looking yet restrained tiles and, if possible, tile the whole room.
- Carpet is fine – hard floors are only essential for letting.
- A shower is a definite plus, but don't ever replace a bath with one; and always fit bath taps with a shower cradle, even when there's a separate shower. Keep fittings classic, as modern designs tend to date.

### Storage space

Well-made, built-in wardrobes, shelves and cupboards (wood, not melamine) make a property easier to sell. Potential buyers like the thought that there'll be somewhere to put things from the moment they move in. Almost every home has neglected corners that could easily be turned into storage space.

### Flooring

Real wooden floors are what people want. Otherwise choose a good-quality wood laminate. Choose neutral shades for carpets. Very pale carpets look classy, but must be spotless.

### Fireplaces

These are always a selling point. Make sure they're in keeping with the style of the property. Real-flame gas fires are popular in flats, but proper grates for real log or coal fires have made a huge comeback in suburban houses.

### Decoration
- Choose neutral colours.
- Avoid patterns on carpets and walls.
- Keep patterns on curtains and upholstery simple and subtle.

The terrible truth about decoration is that beauty is in the eye of the beholder. So let future owners choose their own adventurous colour schemes.

### In general
- Give an impression of light and space – pale walls and a few strategically placed mirrors can help.
- Invest in good-quality door and window furniture.
- All paintwork, inside and out, must be immaculate.
- Good, modern central heating is essential.
- Use concealed spotlights on low ceilings, rather than hanging lights.
- Make unattractive features such as radiators and pipework less noticeable by painting them the same colour as the walls.
- Good security locks on doors and windows, and a burglar alarm (especially in high-crime areas), impress potential buyers.
- There's no need to furnish a newly done-up property if you're not going to live in it, but a few stylish pieces can suggest how the space might be used.

## Profit margins
Do make sure that all your hard work will generate a useful profit – most property developers aim for 20 per cent.
- Find out how much well-modernized similar properties go for in the area.
- Find out how much it will cost you to get the property ready to sell.
- Add together the purchase price and the cost of the works.
- When the work is finished, the selling price should be at least 20 per cent more than the total cost of buying and improving the property.

Example:

| | |
|---|---|
| Purchase price of flat | £120,000 |
| Cost of work | £50,000 |
| Total cost of flat | £170,000 |
| Resale price | £204,000 |
| Gross profit | £34,000 (20 per cent of total outlay) |

When making these calculations be sure to include legal costs and stamp duty in the original purchase price, and any fees you incurred during the improvements.

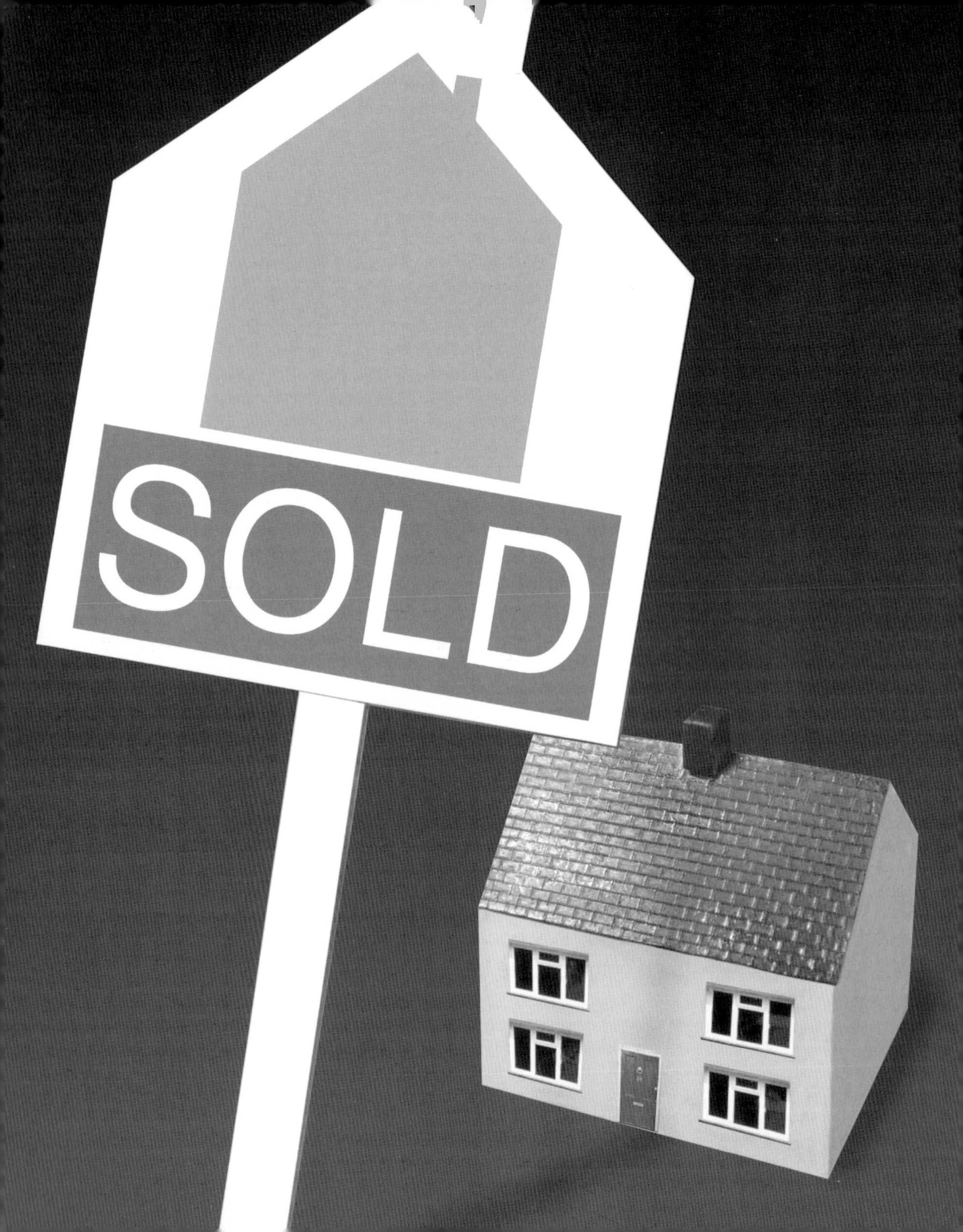
SOLD

# 8

# Selling your home

**There's no escaping the fact that selling is a nail-biting business – doubly so if you're trying to buy at the same time, because the timing is so crucial.** But unless you take off for the Bahamas, leaving the whole matter in the hands of a trusted estate agent, you are going to have to:

- get your home in good order (if it isn't already)
- keep it immaculately clean and tidy for several weeks or months
- put up with hordes of nit-picking strangers traipsing through it
- endure the roller-coaster ride of waiting for an acceptable offer and seeing it through to exchange and completion.

First-time buyers can feel smug here because, for the first and last time in their property-buying lives, none of this applies to them.

# How much is your home worth?

**Your first step, before consulting any agents, is to find out what other similar properties are going for.** Look in the local paper and estate agents' windows and read the property columns to get an idea of the state of the market. The best time to put a property on the market is spring or early autumn.

When you've got a clear idea of what you think your property is worth, get some professional valuations. Remember: you are under no obligation to offer your home for sale through a particular agent just because they have valued it. Ask two or three different ones (there's no charge because they're all hoping to be instructed) and don't tell them in advance what you think your home is worth, though they are sure to ask.

Some agents value high simply because they want the business and then, when the property doesn't sell, suggest you drop the price. Others value low because they've got their eye on a quick and easy commission. So if one estimate is very different from the others, ask the agent his/her reasons. What you want from these valuations is a realistic expert opinion of what your property is worth. And you need to know whether the price quoted is an asking price or what they think the place will actually go for.

All sorts of things have to be taken into account when estimating the value of a property. Architectural style, size, accommodation and general condition are of course important, but location is even more so – not just the area and the road but where the property is positioned in the road, the direction in which it faces and what it looks out on. Every street has its 'ceiling' (the top price that any property there will fetch), but no two properties will be worth exactly the same. The value of yours will depend on how you have looked after it, what you have done to it and how you present it.

# VALUATION — CASE STUDY

During the ten years they lived in their small Victorian house in Bristol, David and Anna P made a lot of imaginative improvements to it. These included turning a dark cellar (once a grocer's storeroom) into a good-size playroom and creating a 22-foot master bedroom in the loft with an en-suite bathroom. They also extended their small galley kitchen into the side patio to make an attractive kitchen–diner.

When the time came to sell, theirs was a difficult property to value because it was the only one in a street of two-up two-downs to have so much additional accommodation. Three different agents valued it at three very different prices: £210,000, £225,000 and £250,000. They themselves, having looked at similar properties in comparable areas of the city, thought it might fetch as much as £275,000.

The problem, according to the agent who had given the lowest valuation, was that their street had a 'ceiling' of around £200,000 and he felt that no house there, however superior, would sell for much more than that. But David and Anna decided to back their hunch and persuaded the agent who had given the highest valuation to put it on the market at £275,000. It was spring, the market was buoyant and within a few weeks they achieved their asking price. 'I know estate agents are supposed to be the experts,' Anna comments, 'but I actually think we had a better idea of who our house would appeal to.'

# Getting ready to sell

**Some sellers with money to burn employ professional 'house doctors' to come in, and redecorate and rearrange before they put their home on the market – and pay around £90 an hour, plus the cost of the work, for the privilege.** It's claimed this can add about 15–20 per cent to the selling price. But a little common-sense can undoubtedly achieve the same thing for a good deal less.

Try to look at your house or flat through someone else's eyes before putting it up for sale. Strong emotions are tied up in a home, so sometimes it's hard to be detached. If that's the case, ask an (honest) friend what they think are the most off-putting features – then see if there's anything you can do about them.

## Essential repairs

Once Home Information Packs (see page 86) become compulsory, we are all going to know a great deal more about the condition of our properties before they go on the market – which will give us the chance to put right any important defects. It is certainly worth repairing or replacing anything that looks obviously ropy:

- cracked windows
- rotten woodwork
- detached or leaking gutters
- peeling wallpaper
- chipped or discoloured paint
- cracked or badly stained sanitaryware
- cracks in woodwork or plaster.

Small internal cracks can easily be filled and painted over; large ones should probably be looked at by a surveyor so you can reassure viewers that there's nothing wrong and, if necessary, show them the report.

## Exterior decoration

Make the outside of your property look like a million dollars because 'kerb appeal' is terrifically important. If people don't like the way your home looks from the outside, they won't bother to view. Give the front door a new coat of paint – royal blue is the preferred colour – and add some shiny brasswork.

## Interior decoration

It's not worth redecorating your whole house or flat just to sell it. Try cleaning the carpets and washing down the walls and woodwork instead. If you feel you've absolutely got to redecorate a room, give it a quick lick of light, neutral emulsion. Look critically at each area of your home.

### Hall

This needs to be light and welcoming. A higher wattage bulb and a smart new lampshade (especially if yours is a paper one that's become discoloured) can make a huge difference. Consider a beautiful glass one – nothing you splash out on is a waste of money if you can take it away with you! Banish bicycles, scooters, Rollerblades, boots and trainers.

### Living room

This crucial room must be displayed to its best advantage. If it's too full of furniture or if the pieces are too bulky, move some out. Clean windows and wash (or, even better, remove) net curtains and don't forget that rugs, throws and hangings can cover a multitude of sins.

### Bedrooms

If redecorating, choose a calm colour – light blue is said to encourage sleep. It's worth investing in a colour-coordinated bedspread or duvet cover and pillowcase. Get rid of clutter and old clothes to make space.

### Bathroom

Remove limescale from baths and loos – easily done with proprietary cleaners – and clean up any signs of mould. Shabby tiles can be improved with grout whitener. A new bath mat and fluffy towels will give your bathroom a fresh look.

### Kitchen

As already mentioned, it's not worth spending a fortune on your kitchen if you're about to sell, though you could consider replacing a vinyl floor if it's particularly worn and dirty. A few stylish new accessories – decorative Mediterranean plates and pottery, tea towels, storage jars – can work wonders.

## Gardens

Nowadays, gardens are seen as rooms in their own right – places to eat, relax and entertain. Beautiful, well-established greenery and flowering plants are always a plus point, although busy career people often prefer low-maintenance gardens, hence the fashion for decking, gravel, water features and pebbles.

There's a lot you can do to give your garden instant buyer-appeal.

- Tubs and pots are the quickest way to add colour. If you haven't got time to plant them up yourself, buy some ready-planted.
- Hanging baskets filled with trailing greenery and flowering bedding plants give a sunny, Mediterranean feel.
- Repair and if necessary repaint fences, gates and trellis-work.
- Tidy and repair the garden shed.
- Clear away all rubbish; remove dog and cat poo.
- Clear weeds from paths and paving, then treat with weedkiller. If nothing's in bloom, buy some bedding plants to dot about.
- Cut lawn edges – this creates an instant appearance of neatness.
- If it's the growing season, mow the lawn – house-buyers like the smell.
- Banish gnomes and other twee garden ornaments to the garage – they may not be to everyone's taste – but leave stone bird-baths and statues.
- Trim hedges, and prune overhanging branches.
- Cover unsightly manhole covers with tubs.
- Smother weeds with the contents of a bag of mulch – compost, bark or coir, but not farmyard manure as it smells.
- Don't use organic fertilizers just before viewers arrive, for the same reason.
- Feed the lawn – it will go green within two weeks.
- Invest in rustic-looking garden furniture – after all, you can take it with you.

### Front gardens

These are especially crucial when you are trying to sell a property because they're the first thing people see. Mend the front gate, clean the front path, clear away weeds, rubbish and bins, put plants in tubs, pots and window boxes. Consider covering neglected patches with gravel or pebbles.

## Create good vibes

You don't have to believe in feng shui (the ancient Chinese art of arranging objects in a way that is meant to attract good fortune) in order to recognize that where you place things can have a huge effect on the overall 'feel' of a home. Forget wind chimes, crystals and fish tanks, but do:

- avoid clutter – it depresses people
- reflect light and nice views with mirrors
- mend, hide or dump anything that looks broken/messy/neglected
- keep pathways to doors and windows clear
- keep windows sparkling clean
- display fresh plants and flowers. Silk or dried ones are fine in dark corners, but only if they haven't gathered the dust of years.

# Selling through an agent

**Around three-quarters of all vendors use an estate agent – either because they believe an agent will achieve a higher price or because they are unwilling or too busy to market the property themselves.**

The main advantage of selling through an agent is that he/she can take some of the work and worry off your shoulders. He/she will:

- value your home and agree an asking price
- prepare professional-looking details to send out to applicants
- contact would-be buyers who might be interested
- probably reach a wider range of buyers than you could on your own
- sort out genuine buyers from time-wasters
- show people round when you are not at home
- accompany viewers, even when you are at home
- keep advertising your property in the local press and, often, the Internet
- negotiate a purchase price for you
- send you and your buyer a memorandum confirming what you have agreed
- be a link between you, your buyer and your solicitor right up to completion.

But estate agents charge a commission of between 1.5 and 3.5 per cent of the purchase price, which usually amounts to several thousand pounds. Normally it's around 2 per cent if they are the only agent selling the house (sole agency) or around 3 per cent if you have instructed more than one agent (multiple agency) – in which case whichever agent sells the house gets the fee. Occasionally two agents agree to be 'joint sole agents', which means that they share the commission regardless of which one sells the property. Normally, no commission is due if an agent fails to sell a property – but never give an agent 'sole selling rights' as this deceptive little phrase is not the same as 'sole agency' and you would have to pay the full commission even if you find a buyer yourself.

# Choosing an agent

When you're on a tight budget a difference of half a per cent in commission is likely to influence you, but bear in mind that a good estate agent who attracts a lot of applicants may earn their higher commission by selling your property more quickly and achieving a higher price for it.

As with any other profession, there are good estate agents, average estate agents and appalling estate agents. Horror stories still abound, but things have improved considerably since a code of practice was introduced in 1998. All members of the National Association of Estate Agents and Royal Institute of Chartered Surveyors must abide by this code.

The main points of the code of practice are:

- Agents must not discriminate against anyone because of their race, creed, gender, disability or nationality
- Agents must not harass people in order to gain instructions to sell a property
- Agents must tell clients if there is any conflict of interest – for example, if a buyer is a friend or associate
- Agents must give clients written confirmation of instructions, including terms, fees and expenses, before they commit
- Agents must give truthful valuations based on the state of the market, and not misrepresent the value of a property in order to gain an instruction
- 'For Sale' boards can be erected only with the client's permission
- Written details of a property must be accurate and be sent to the seller for their approval
- Agents must tell clients of all offers that have been made for the property. They should not treat offers differently, holding back one in favour of another, or misrepresent rival offers to a buyer
- Agents must not discriminate against buyers who don't want to use their financial services
- Agents must take reasonable steps to establish that a would-be purchaser has the funds to buy
- After an offer has been accepted, the buyer must be told if the seller wishes to keep the property on the market until contracts have been exchanged (so the buyer knows there is the possibility of being gazumped)
- Agents must accompany applicants on viewings (before the code was introduced, many agents simply sent applicants round to be shown the property by the vendor)
- Agents must also never give the prospective buyer the keys to a property.

# Before instructing an agent

Putting your property in the hands of the right agent will greatly increase your chances of achieving a quick, smooth sale, so take a little time to check out all possible candidates before making your final choice.

- Look in their window to make sure they deal with your kind of property.
- Ask how they advertise. You want someone who takes a prominent, full-colour page in the local paper every week and has an efficient website.
- Make sure your property would feature regularly. Some agents advertise each property only once or only advertise a certain type of property.
- Count the number of boards – especially 'Sold' boards – they have in your area.
- Make sure their office is in a prominent high-street position, where lots of potential purchasers will see it.
- Find out about their standard of service. Some wily sellers get a friend or relative to register with them to discover just how helpful and efficient they really are.
- Check that they belong to a recognized professional association (NAEA, RICS, ASI or ABE).
- Compare their charges with those of other local agents.

Don't choose an agent just because they've put a leaflet through your door claiming that they've just sold a 'similar property in your street' and have 'a number of disappointed applicants' waiting to snap yours up. Although this could be true, it is a very well-known way of touting for business. Ask which property they sold, how long it took and whether any of the disappointed applicants is in a position to buy. Even better, you could ask the owners of the property they sold (if it really is similar to yours) what the agents were like to deal with and whether they (the vendors) were aware of any disappointed applicants. Quite apart from having confidence in an agent's ability to sell your property, it's important to get along with them and like the way they do business.

Once you have instructed an agent, keep in close touch and discuss how things are going. If hardly any people come to view, it could be because the market is quiet or it may be because the agent isn't trying hard enough. If lots of people are coming but none of the viewers is making a serious offer, you need to discuss what's putting them off and whether the price is right. It is easy to change agents, but you must leave your property with them for the agreed time – perhaps six weeks. It's unwise to keep changing agents as your property will, rightly or wrongly, acquire a reputation for being difficult to sell.

# ESTATE AGENTS – A CAUTIONARY TALE

Despite the code of practice, estate agency is a cut-throat business. Derek G, a flat-owner in Barnes, west London, decided to change sole agents because he felt the ones he had instructed (Agent A) were not doing a good job. Little did he know that before he disinstructed them, and while he was away, they had shown around his flat a couple who, two months later, viewed the flat again through his new agents (Agent B), but didn't mention they had seen it before. After the couple bought the flat through Agent B, Agent A claimed the full sole-agency fee for 'introducing' them. Since Derek could afford to pay only one lot of commission, and Agent A refused to share it with Agent B, the case went to court and the sum was eventually divided between the two agents.

While all this was going on, Derek needed to view a house that, as luck would have it, was being sold by Agent A. Because the agent repeatedly ignored his telephone requests for a viewing, Derek popped a note through the letter box of the house, explaining the situation and asking if he could view it privately. The owners agreed and Derek bought the property. But Agent A still claimed the commission and, faced with threats of legal action, the vendors caved in because it would have been impossible to prove that Agent A had ignored requests for a viewing.

Unfortunately, this kind of thing is not as rare as it should be and illustrates, first, the importance of making sure your agent tells you the name of every single applicant who views your house, just in case the same name crops up again through another agent; and, second, that hell hath no fury like an agent who has been bypassed, however valid the reasons.

# Selling without an agent

**If you market your home yourself, you will have to show buyers around (not a good idea if you live alone) and negotiate the selling price.** Not everyone is suited to the task – you need patience, good judgement, organizational skills and some financial know-how. But if you are successful, you will save a lot of money.

Some people decide to go it alone for six to eight weeks and then instruct an agent if they've had no luck. If the market is buoyant, and you think yours is an easy property to sell, it's certainly worth giving it a go. If so, you will have to:

- get your home ready to sell
- ask two or three agents to value it
- fix an asking price
- draw up some particulars
- advertise the property as widely as possible.

## Preparing your own property details

Printed details are not essential if you are doing your own selling, but it's useful to have some to give to people who respond to your initial advertisement.

- Take some good photographs of the outside of your home and of any particularly attractive features – garden, living room, kitchen. You can either glue these on the particulars or, if you have a digital camera, incorporate them into the details on your computer, to print out or e-mail.
- Take accurate measurements of every room.
- Write a clear, brief general description of your home – the type of building, the number of bedrooms and any other important information. Include good selling-points such as 'quiet, tree-lined road', 'five minutes' walk from station' or 'recently modernized', and remember to mention plus points such as a new boiler, double-glazing or cavity-wall insulation – but don't be tempted to oversell or misrepresent anything.
- Briefly describe each room. Include the measurements, what it looks out on and any permanent fixtures and fittings.
- Describe the garden, garage and any outbuildings.
- Mention items such as curtains that you are willing to sell separately.
- Say whether the property is freehold or leasehold. If leasehold, state how many years are left on the lease and what the service charge is.

- State the price.
- Include directions for finding the property.

## Where to advertise
- Put a double-sided 'For Sale' sign outside your property – this must be no bigger than 0.5 square metres. It's probably best to get one made professionally (this costs about £50) unless you're good at woodwork and lettering. Say 'Viewings by appointment only' and give a phone number.
- Place cards in local shop windows and on notice boards.
- Put classified ads in a selection of appropriate publications: local papers, free-ad papers or (if your property is upmarket or unusual) national daily or Sunday papers. The nationals are expensive, so try local papers and ad magazines first, and take one of the package deals (five ads for the cost of three, etc.) as single advertisements are not cost-effective. Some free-ad papers also offer a property-selling package that includes a 'For Sale' board, an information pack and a free legal helpline.
- Workplace notice-boards and house magazines can be very effective.
- Try a property shop. These look like estate agents, but all they do is display details and, in some cases, computer-match properties with potential buyers. You pay a fixed fee based on the price of your property.

## Wording your advertisement
Your initial advertisement needs to be brief and to the point. Start with an eye-catching adjective such as 'spacious', 'stunning', 'charming' or 'well-modernized', and then state the type of property. Give as much useful information as you can without resorting to a list of abbreviations. The ad should include:
- the number of bedrooms, living rooms and bathrooms
- central heating
- length of garden
- the approximate location ('near Pleasantville Station')
- the price and a phone number.

If you take a display advertisement in a paper you will have space to say more and even include a photo.

## Property websites
In addition to estate agents' own websites, there are now more than 50 websites that allow you to market your home without an estate agent. Some are free, while others charge various fees depending on the type of service you choose. The cost of advertising online is so low that you could consider doing this as well as

instructing a sole agent. Selling online is legally the same as a private sale, because a property website is not classed as an 'agent', so you would not be breaking any agreement. And if you find a buyer before your agent does you could save yourself a tidy sum. Most sites charge a fixed fee of around £50 to £100 to advertise your property until it sells. What you get for this varies from site to site. The cheapest deals give you a standard advert with a single photo, while others include a 'For Sale' board, free digital photographs of your property and even press advertisements. For quite a lot more (around £300), your ad can include a virtual tour of your home.

Advantages of advertising online:

- It's cheap (in some cases free)
- You can combine it with using an estate agent
- Your property description can go online within two hours of being entered
- You can amend your ad at any time – change the price or the description
- Prospective buyers contact you directly by e-mail or phone
- (In some cases) prospective buyers receive an e-mail if your property matches their search
- The people who bother to contact you are probably serious buyers.

Before signing up to a property website:

- Research the market to find out which sites advertise your kind of property in your area (some focus only on London or inside the M25)
- Choose a site with good presentation that offers easy navigation tools
- Check out the competition to see if you are getting the best deal
- Describe your property carefully and be as accurate as possible
- For security reasons don't give your full name and address – just give a first name and e-mail address or mobile number (and see the following section).

## Security

Whatever method of advertising you've used:

- Don't invite anyone to come and view your property without getting their name, phone number (and, if possible, address) first. Make sure these are genuine by saying you will call the person back to arrange a time
- Arrange viewings during daylight hours only
- If people turn up at your door on spec, make an appointment for them to come back. If they don't keep it you will know they weren't serious
- If you feel at all uncomfortable about showing the property on your own, arrange to have a friend or relative present
- Find out about the person's buying situation – do they have a property to sell? Have they put it on the market or is it under offer?

# Handling the viewings

**It pays to do a little preparation for each viewing.** A 'they can take us as they find us' approach is all very well, but it won't help you to sell your property. Your overall plan should be to create the impression of a lovingly cared-for home, in which you and yours have been living a calm, happy, well-organized life!

DO:

- Store clutter where it won't fall out on viewers if they open a cupboard – in storage boxes under the bed, perhaps
- Ventilate the house or flat and use air-fresheners if you smoke or have pets. Smell is important, but the aroma of home-baked bread or freshly brewed coffee is such a well-known ploy that it might seem obvious. Try aromatherapy instead – the essential oils of clary sage and lemon are said to make people feel comfortable. Soak a ball of cotton wool in the oil and leave it in a warm place, or use a vaporizer
- Have soft classical music playing (it sounds corny, but it impresses potential buyers)
- Leave a good light on in dark rooms
- Empty and clear out your garage. Your car should be outside it, preferably gleaming (if it's falling apart, park it round the corner and borrow a friend's Mercedes)
- Make sure all the beds are made (and no one is in them)
- Remove dustbins from the front of the property
- Clean the bathroom, tidy away personal items and leave the loo seat down
- Put any money, jewellery or valuables out of sight
- Farm out noisy, demanding children and pets
- Put fresh flowers or a plant in the entrance hall.

DON'T:

- Leave the TV on or have loud music playing
- Have strong-smelling food cooking (or recently cooked)
- Leave used plates, cups, glasses or half-eaten food lying around
- Leave cooking debris in the kitchen – potato peelings, greasy frying pans, overflowing waste bins (but do put a bowl of fresh fruit on the table)
- Leave cat-litter trays on view
- Leave embarrassing personal items or dubious videos and magazines lying about.

## Showing your home to prospective buyers

It's quite unnerving to have strangers poking around your home, so it helps to develop a detached attitude. If the buyer is accompanied by an agent, just let them get on with it – don't follow them around.

If you are selling without an agent and are showing people the property yourself, your manner should be friendly and relaxed but businesslike. Give them a brief guided tour, pointing out all the nicest features, but don't oversell. High-pressure sales techniques or pushiness will just make the viewer want to turn tail and run. Allow them space to absorb the atmosphere and take in details and, when you've shown them round once, ask if they'd like to wander round again on their own (but use your judgement and don't let them do so if you have any doubts).

Afterwards, ask if they have any queries. Some viewers may ask quite daft or intrusive questions, but keep smiling – you only have to say as much as you want. If they seem interested, invite them to come back for a second viewing. Make sure they have the particulars you have prepared and give them your phone number if they don't already have it.

Some do-it-yourself sellers also prepare a small information pack (not to be confused with an official Home Information Pack) to show interested viewers. This might include:

- any guarantees for timber treatment or damp-proofing
- receipts for major outlays like a new boiler or roof insulation
- recent bills – council tax, electricity, gas or oil
- information about local transport, schools, shops, churches, parks or sports facilities
- a surveyor's report on anything that looks dubious.

# The selling process

**A natural question after all these preparations is, 'How long will it take to sell my property?'** The only answer to this is: how long is a piece of string?

Don't expect the first person who comes to look at your home to buy it – this would be very unusual. Also, it's hard to judge from someone's enthusiasm whether they are really a potential buyer. Some people walk round in total silence, then surprise you by making an offer. Others gush and admire everything, then vanish without trace. Sometimes one half of a couple comes to see a property and is very keen, then the other half sees it and is not remotely interested. Estate agents say it tends to be the woman who decides (because men don't really care where they live!). In general, you should expect to show quite a few people your home before finding a buyer, although during property booms houses and flats often get snapped up the day they come on the market.

## Dealing with offers

This is where an estate agent comes in handy, as he or she should have a shrewd idea of whether a buyer's offer is genuine. When you receive an acceptable offer, the first thing you need to know is whether the buyer is in a position to proceed.

- Do they have a property to sell and is it under offer?
- Do they have a mortgage arranged in principle? (If possible, find out what proportion of the price they are borrowing, as if it's very high and the lender down-values the property, they may have to back out.)
- Are they being held up by a chain?
- When do they want to complete?

On no account accept an offer from someone who hasn't sold their own property, because if you take your home off the market you will miss out on other buyers who are ready to proceed. But by all means stay in touch with them as their situation could change at any time.

## Low offers

Your response to a low offer will depend on how long the property has been on the market and how desperate you are to sell. Unless it's a truly insulting offer, don't dismiss it out of hand. Consider:

- Is the buyer just trying it on?
- Are they likely to up the offer – a lot, or a little?
- Are you likely to get a better one from someone else?
- Have you pitched your price too high?
- Could you afford to proceed with your proposed purchase at this price?
- Can you afford to lose this buyer?

Purchase prices are seldom agreed in the first round, but you don't want to keep haggling, especially over relatively small sums, because this creates resentment. Ask the buyer to justify his/her low offer and give your own reasons for believing the property is worth more. Sometimes it makes sense simply to tell the buyer (or your agent) the lowest price you're prepared to accept. If there is not too much difference between you, you will probably reach an agreement.

## After acceptance

It's normal to take a property off the market after you have accepted an offer, providing the would-be purchaser is ready to buy and has given you or your agent the name of their solicitor. Some sellers ask for a small returnable deposit at this stage, though there's not really much point. If you are selling the property yourself, send the buyer a memorandum of everything you have agreed:

- the address of the property
- the purchase price
- fixtures and fittings included in the sale
- anything you have agreed to sell separately
- your name
- the buyer's name
- both solicitors' names and contact details
- the proposed completion date.

Send this with a letter, but don't sign the sale agreement itself. Even though signing would not make the agreement a legally binding document, it's best to avoid even the smallest risk of this.

## Surveys

The first real sign that your buyer is proceeding with the purchase comes when an appointment is made for their (or their lender's) surveyor/valuer to inspect the property. This normally happens within two or three weeks, so if it doesn't, ask why. It could simply be that the lender is being inefficient or the surveyor is on holiday, but it's also possible that your buyer's mortgage application has run into trouble, and you need to know about this as early as possible so you don't waste time when you could be finding another buyer.

Prepare for the survey as you would for a viewing. First impressions count, even with surveyors, so everything should look clean, tidy and cared for. If it's just a valuation, the surveyor will probably spend only half an hour so looking around (less, if it's a small flat) but a full structural survey will take several hours.

The purpose of a valuation is make sure that the property is worth what the buyer is paying for it (and at least much as the mortgage provider is lending), while a survey looks to see if there are any structural or other defects that are likely to reduce its value in the near future or cost the buyer a lot of money.

Problems arise for you, the seller, if the property is down-valued or if any unexpected defects are discovered, as the buyer will use these as an excuse to renegotiate the purchase price or even pull out of the sale. You should ask to see the report, as the surveyor may simply have recommended that something should be repaired in the fairly near future, or that an expert opinion should be sought. Or he may have advised the lender to hold back some of the advance until certain specified work is done. This kind of thing is not really a reason for dropping the price and you are under no obligation to do so.

If you think the survey is overcautious or biased, it may be worth getting another professional opinion on the problem, as this might reassure your buyer or any future buyer. You can also use a builder's estimate as ammunition, if the problem wouldn't cost much to put right, or you could promise to get the repair done yourself before exchange. This might be the best solution if a drop in price would mean you couldn't proceed with your own purchase.

By now you should have some idea of how keen your buyer is. If they're extremely keen, they'll probably go ahead anyway, though they may still push for a price reduction. But if they think the property is going to cost them more than they can afford they will walk away unless they can make their sums add up. Sometimes it's worth agreeing to a small reduction just to keep the buyer happy. But watch out for gazundering. If a buyer comes up with some spurious reason for paying less when you are about to exchange contracts, just say no.

One of the great advantages of Home Information Packs, when they eventually come in, will be that buyers will know everything there is to know about a property before they make an offer, so there should never be any need to renegotiate.

## Completing your sale

The legal side of selling a property is less complicated than buying because the buyer's solicitor does most of the work. You will have to fill in any forms that your solicitor sends you and provide evidence of such things as service charges, building-regulations certificates and past planning permissions. As with buying, keep in close touch with your solicitor or conveyancer throughout the transaction and, when completion day comes, don't part with your keys until they tell you the money has been transferred.

Between exchange and completion your buyer is likely to want to come and measure, or bring a builder to give an estimate. As a safeguard, either you or your estate agent should be there for these visits. If the property is empty, you may feel you trust your buyer enough to lend them the keys – this is entirely up to you. But your estate agent should never hand over the keys without your permission. On the day you move out, it is a courtesy to leave your home looking spick and span – although troublesome buyers should not be too surprised if this has been overlooked!

## Final Word

In an ideal world buying and selling a home would be a smoother and easier process than it is at the moment. But forewarned is forearmed and, hopefully, this book has taken the mystery out of the technicalities, and equipped you to make the very best choices. With luck, your property deal will run like clockwork. But even if, as happens to the best of us, there are moments when you are tearing your hair out, at least you will be in a position to avoid unnecessary expense and keep maximum control of the situation.

A new home is a new life. Enjoy your move!

# Glossary

**advance** the mortgage loan

**assured shorthold tenancy** tenancy agreement whereby the landlord can repossess the property after six months if the correct notice is given

**balance outstanding** the amount of a loan owed at a particular time

**bridging loan** a loan taken out so a buyer can complete a purchase before receiving the proceeds from a sale

**capped-rate mortgage** a mortgage with a top limit set on the interest rate

**chain** when several people are dependent on one another's sales to complete their purchases

**charge (or legal charge)** a right to repayment from the proceeds of selling a property

**completion date** the date when the money is paid and the buyer moves in

**contract** the written agreement to sell/buy a property

**conveyancing** the legal process of transferring land or a building from one owner to another

**covenant** an undertaking to do or not do certain things with a property

**current-account mortgage (CAM)** a flexible mortgage in which the credit balance on your current account is offset against the outstanding balance of your mortgage loan in order to reduce the amount of interest due

**deeds** legal document entitling you to a property

**disbursements** money paid out by your solicitor on your behalf during conveyancing

**discharge** paying off a mortgage

**discount mortgage** a mortgage that starts with reduced payments over an an agreed period

**early redemption** paying off a loan before the end of the term

**early redemption penalty** financial penalty incurred when a loan is repaid early

**endowment mortgage** an interest-only mortgage linked to an investment which is designed to pay off the capital at the end of the loan period

**equity** the difference between the value of your home and the amount of your mortgage

**exchange of contracts** the moment when an agreement to buy/sell a property becomes legally binding

**fixed rate** an interest rate that remains the same for an agreed period

**flexible mortgage** a mortgage that allows over- and underpayments and payment holidays

**freehold** property owned absolutely until the end of time

**gazumping** when a vendor accepts a higher offer after agreeing a sale

**gazundering** when a buyer reduces their offer just before contracts are due to be exchanged

**ground rent** annual sum paid by a leaseholder to a freeholder

**Home Information Pack** a pack giving information about title, searches, survey and terms of sale, which, when brought in (possibly in 2006), will speed up property transactions

**housing association** non-profit-making organization that provides low rent and shared-ownership housing

**interest-only mortgage** a mortgage in which the monthly payments consist of interest but no capital. There is normally another scheme to pay off the capital

**ISA mortgage** an interest-only mortgage linked to an Individual Savings Account

**joint tenancy** when two people hold half shares in a property; if one dies the other automatically takes the whole

**land certificate** a certificate from the Land Registry which proves ownership of a house

**leasehold** the ownership of a property for a fixed number of years

**Loan to Value (LTV)** the percentage of a property's value that is being borrowed as a mortgage

**local search** application to the local authority for details on a particular property

**memorandum of sale** a summary of the terms and conditions of a sale as first agreed

**missives** the exchange of letters that creates a binding contract under Scottish law

**mortgage** a loan secured by property

**Mortgage Indemnity Guarantee (MIG)** insurance policy which protects the lender in the event that a property is sold for less than the amount of the mortgage

**mortgage-protection policy** insurance policy that covers mortgage repayments in the event of redundancy, illness or accident, and pays off the mortgage in the case of the borrower's death

**mortgage retention** when a lender holds back part of the mortgage loan until certain works have been carried out

**mortgagee** the lender

**mortgagor** the borrower

**negative equity** when a property is worth less than the amount borrowed to buy it

**pension mortgage** an interest-only mortgage in which the loan is repaid by savings put into a pension plan

**preliminary enquiries** questions the seller has to answer before exchange of contracts

**probate sale** the sale of a property after the owner has died

**redemption** paying off a loan

**registered land** land of which the ownership is registered at the Land Registry

**remortgage** taking out a new or bigger mortgage on the same property

**repayment mortgage** a loan on which the capital as well as the interest is repaid through the term of the loan

**repossession** when a mortgage lender takes a property away from the borrower and sells it to repay the mortgage debt

**retention** holding back part of a mortgage loan until certain repairs have been satisfactorily completed

**stamp duty** a tax levied by the government on all property purchases over £60,000

**subject to contract** term use to describe an agreement that is not yet legally binding

**SVR** standard variable rate of interest that moves up and down with the base rate

**tenants in common** joint owners who own equal or unequal shares in a property. Each is free to dispose of their share in any way they wish

**title** ownership of property

**title deeds** documents proving ownership of land

**tracker mortgage** mortgage with an interest rate that tracks the base rate

**transfer deed** the Land Registry document that transfers the legal ownership of property

**under offer** indicates that a sale has been agreed subject to contract

**vacant possession** the vacant, unoccupied state of a property on completion day

**vendor** the seller

# Useful contacts

## Architects
- The Architects Registration Board 020 7580 5861 www.arb.org.uk
- Architectural Association 020 7887 4000 www.aaschool.ac.uk
- Architecture and Surveying Institute (now incorporated in the Chartered Institute of Building) 01344 630 798 www.ciob.org.uk
- Royal Incorporation of Architects in Scotland 0131 229 7545 www.rias.org.uk
- Royal Institute of British Architects 020 7580 5533 www.riba.org
- Royal Society of Architects in Wales 029 2087 4753 www.architecture-wales.com
- Royal Society of Ulster Architects 028 9032 3760 www.rsua.org.uk

## Building engineers
- Association of Building Engineers 01604 404 121 www.abe.org.uk

## Building regulators
- Construction Confederation www.constructionconfederation. co.uk 020 7608 5000
- Federation of Master Builders 020 7242 7583 www.fmb.org.uk
- House Builders' Federation 020 7608 5100 www.hbf.co.uk
- National Federation of Builders 020 7608 5150 www.builders.org.uk

- National House Building Council 01494 735 363 www.nhbc.co.uk

## Banks & building societies
- Building Societies Association 020 7437 0655 www.bsa.org.uk
- Building Societies Ombudsman 020 7931 0044
- Financial Ombudsman Service 0845 080 1800 www.obo.org.uk

## Chartered surveyors
- Royal Institution of Chartered Surveyors 0870 333 1600 www.rics.org.uk
- Royal Institute of Chartered Surveyors for Scotland www.rics-scotland.org.uk

## Conveyancing
- Council for Licensed Conveyancers 01245 349 599 www.conveyancers.gov.uk

## Electrical contractors
- Electrical Contractors' Association 020 7313 4800 www.eca.co.uk

## Estate agents
- The National Association of Estate Agents 01926 496 800 www.naea.co.uk

## Financial advisers
- IFA Promotion 0117 971 1177 www.unbiased.co.uk

## Gas installation
- CORGI (Council for Registered Gas Installers) 01256 372 200 www.corgi-gas.com

## Glazing
- Glass and Glazing Federation 020 7403 7177 www.ggf.org.uk

## Government bodies
- Office of the Deputy Prime Minister, Housing Private Sector Division www.housing.odpm.gov.uk
- Office for the Ombudsman of Estate Agents 01722 333 306 www.oea.co.uk
- The Planning Inspectorate 0117 372 6372 www.planning-inspectorate.gov.uk

## Historic properties
- CADW (Welsh Heritage) 0292 500 200 www.cadw.wales.gov.uk
- English Heritage 020 7973 3000 www.english-heritage.org.uk
- Environment and Heritage Service (Northern Ireland) 02890 235 000 www.ehsni.gov.uk
- Historic Scotland 0131 668 8600 www.historic-scotland.gov.uk
- Society for the Protection of Ancient Buildings (SPAB) 020 7377 1644 www.spab.org.uk

## Housing associations

• The Housing Corporation
020 7393 2000
www.housingcorp.gov.uk

## Insurance

• Association of British Insurers
020 7600 3333
www.abi.org.uk

## Legal matters

• The Law Society  020 7242 1222
www.lawsociety.org.uk
• The Law Society of Scotland
0131 226 7411
www.lawscot.org.uk
• Legal Services Ombudsman
0845 601 0794  www.olso.org
• The National Solicitors' Network
020 7370 0245
www.solicitor.co.uk
• Office for the Supervision of
Solicitors  0845 608 6565
www.lawsociety.org.uk
• Scottish Legal Services
Ombudsman  0131 556 9123
www.slso.org.uk

## Leaseholds

• The Leasehold Advisory Service
020 7253 2043
www.lease-advice.org

## Managing/letting agents

• Association of Residential
Managing Agents  020 7978 2607
www.arma.org.uk
• Association of Residential Letting
Agents  0845 345 5752
www.arla.co.uk

## Mortgage regulation

• Council of Mortgage Lenders
020 7437 0075
www.cml.org.uk
• Mortgage Code Compliance
Board www.mortgagecode.co.uk

## Plumbing/heating/ventilating

• Association of Plumbing and
Heating Contractors
02476 470 626
www.aphc.co.uk
• Heating and Ventilating
Contractors' Association
020 7313 4900
www.hvca.org.uk
• The Institute of Plumbing
01708 472 791
www.registeredplumber.com

## Relocation services

• The Association of Relocation
Agents
08700 737 475
www.relocationagents.com

## Removals/storage

• The British Association of
Removers  020 8861 3331
www.barmovers.com
• National Guild of Removers
and Storers  01494 792 279
www.ngrs.org.uk

## Self-build

• Associated Self-Build Architects
0800 387 310
www.asba-architects.org
• Buildstore  0870 870 9991
www.buildstore.co.uk

## Valuers/auctioneers

• Incorporated Society of Valuers
and Auctioneers see Royal
Institution of Chartered Surveyors

## Windows/conservatories

• National Replacement Window/
Conservatory Advisory Service
0800 028 5809
www.nrwas.org

## Wood preserving and damp-proofing

• British Wood Preserving and
Damp-proofing Association
01332 225 100
www.bwpda.co.uk
• The Guarantee Protection Trust
01494 447 049
www.gptprotection,co.uk

## Websites

**Legal fact sheets online**
www.freelawyer.co.uk
**Mortgage information**
www.about-mortgages.co.uk
www.charcolonline.co.uk
www.moneyfacts.co.uk
www.moneysupermarket.co.uk
www.yourmortgage.co.uk
**Property search (selected)**
www.easier.co.uk
www.findaproperty.com
www.fish4.co.uk
www.homeownersales.co.uk
www.houseweb.co.uk
www.loot.com
www.propertybroker.co.uk
www.thelittlehousecompany.co.uk
www.thisislondon.co.uk

# Index